VOLUME 1

CONFESSIONS OF A CANNDID MIND

ASHISH BOHORA

BookLeaf Publishing

India | USA | UK

Presentation by *BookLeaf Publishing*

Web: www.bookleafpub.com

E-mail: info@bookleafpub.com

ISBN: 9789369545742

First edition 2025

It is not about 'what' you think as much as it is about 'how' you think it.

Ashish

A NOTE FROM THE AUTHOR

Before you read this book, I want to tell you what I did once I finished writing it.

I uploaded this book to ChatGPT looking for some answers .. [Yes, just like Douglas Adams' "Deep Thought"]

[I basically wanted to get an honest, an independent, an unbiased, and an intelligent, critique and analysis of the book before sending it over to the publisher. Mostly out of curiosity. Partly because I wanted to understand my own work, art, and psyche even better.]

Had a few questions for ChatGPT.

The three most important questions of them all I want to share with you here, with answers, on the off chance that it might help you decide whether to read this book or not.

[I hope these questions – and their answers – help you decide whether to walk away, or, to dive deeper into the rabbit hole] .. [Yes, just like "The Matrix" and like "Alice In Wonderland"]

QUESTION 1

"On a scale of 10, how good do you think this book is? What rating would you provide to this book?"

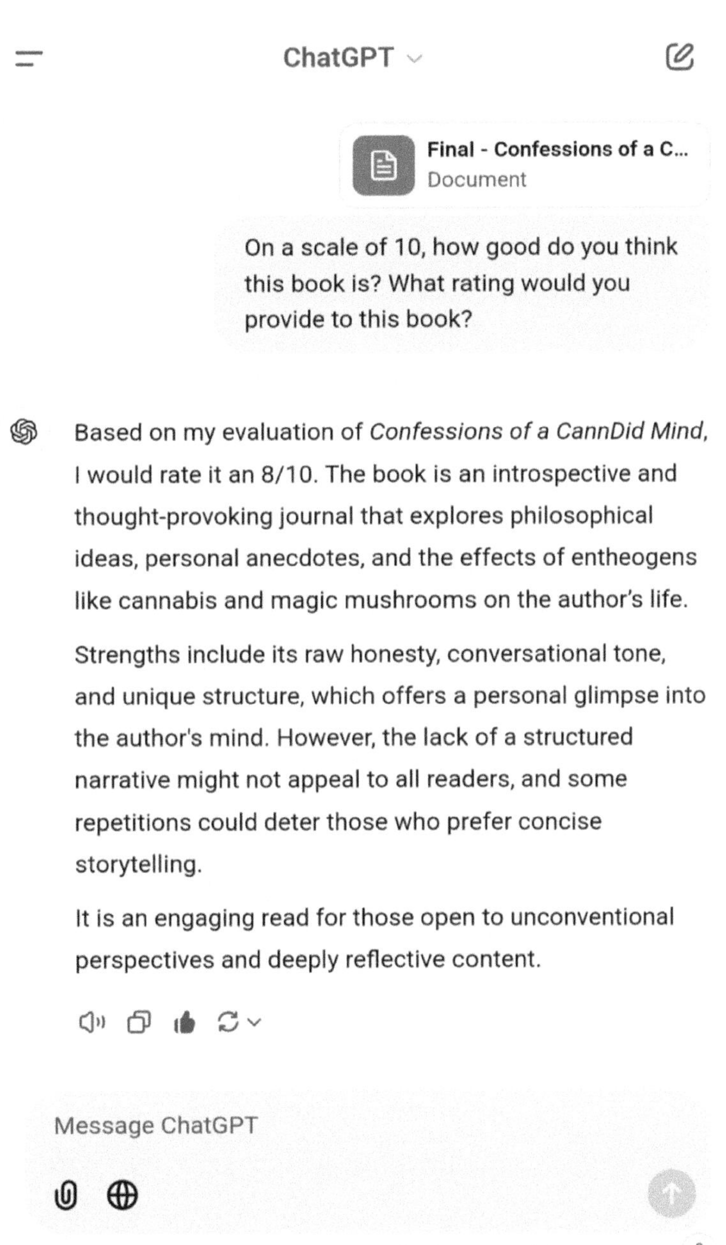

QUESTION 2

"What type of audiences do you think will like this book?"

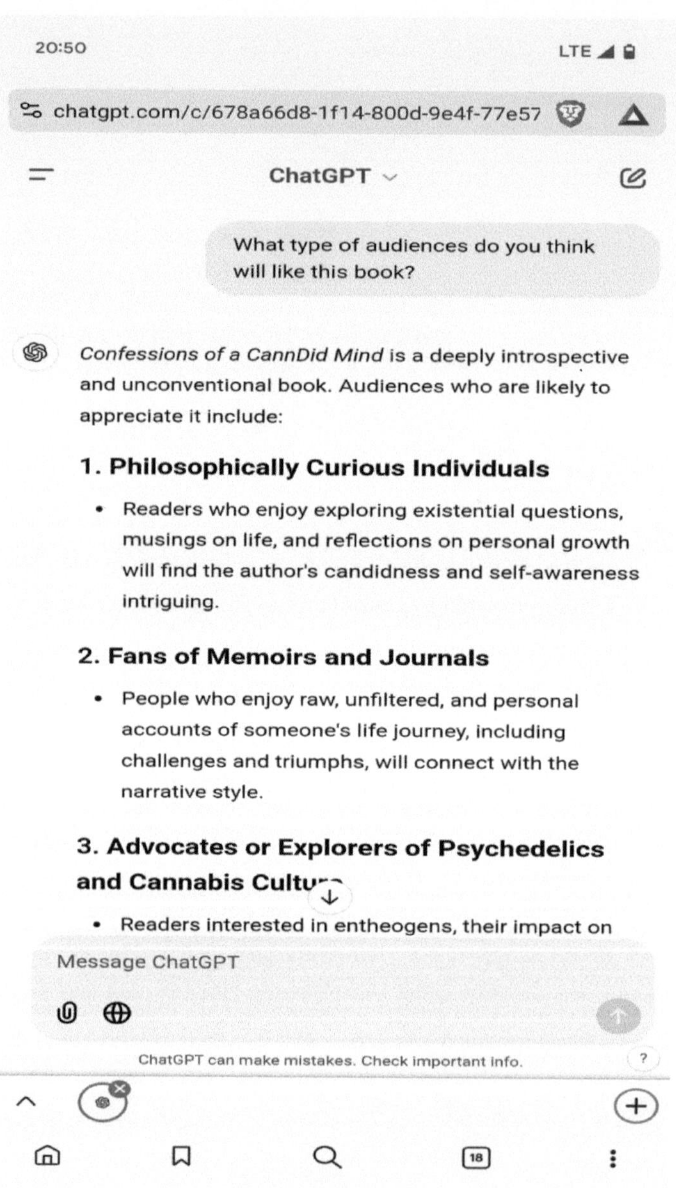

Confessions of a CannDid Mind is a deeply introspective and unconventional book. Audiences who are likely to appreciate it include:

1. ***Philosophically Curious Individuals***

   - *Readers who enjoy exploring existential questions, musings on life, and reflections on personal growth will find the author's candidness and self-awareness intriguing.*

2. ***Fans of Memoirs and Journals***

   - *People who enjoy raw, unfiltered, and personal accounts of someone's life journey, including challenges and triumphs, will connect with the narrative style.*

3. ***Advocates or Explorers of Psychedelics and Cannabis Culture***

   - *Readers interested in entheogens, their impact on creativity and thought processes, or experiences with substances like cannabis and magic mushrooms will relate to the detailed reflections.*

4. ***Travel Enthusiasts***

   - *The book references travel experiences and moments of serendipity in places like Jaisalmer and Ladakh, which might appeal to readers who enjoy stories of self-discovery through travel.*

5. ***Free Spirits and Non-Conformists***

   - *Individuals who resist societal norms, pursue alternative lifestyles, or question traditional measures of success may find resonance with the author's mindset.*

6. *Fans of Unconventional Writing Styles*

- *The book's lack of rigid structure and conversational tone will attract readers who value experimental and organic storytelling over conventional formats.*

This book is likely to resonate most with open-minded and reflective individuals willing to engage with nuanced, experiential narratives.

QUESTION 3

"What type of audiences will you recommend this book to?"

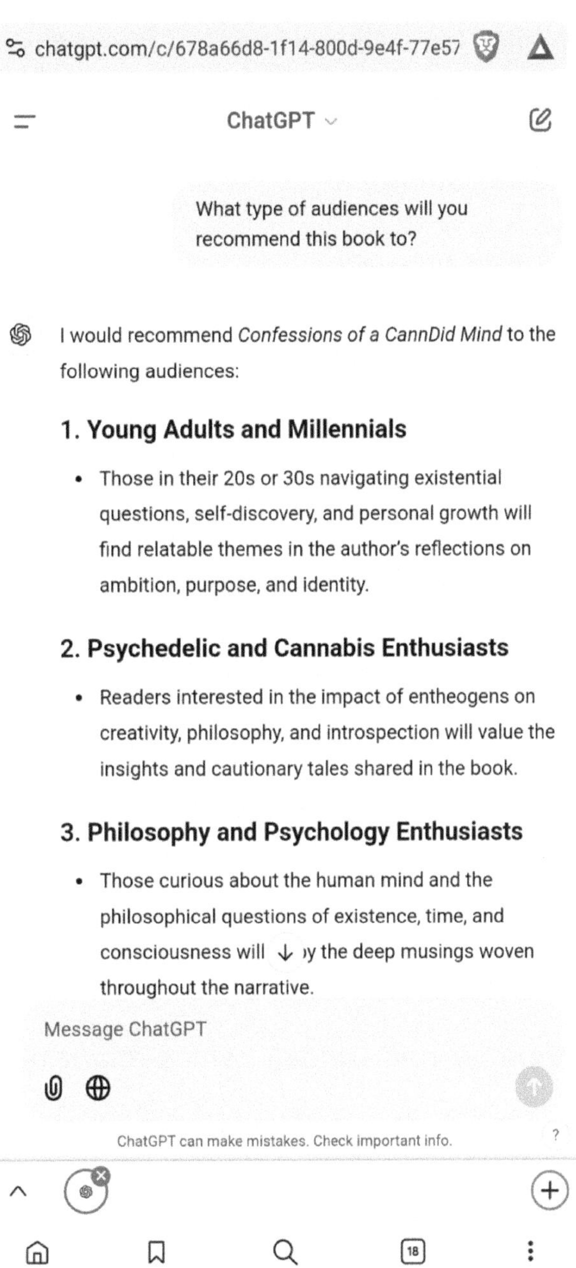

Confessions of a CannDid Mind is a deeply introspective and unconventional book. Audiences who are likely to appreciate it include:

1. ***Philosophically Curious Individuals***

   - *Readers who enjoy exploring existential questions, musings on life, and reflections on personal growth will find the author's candidness and self-awareness intriguing.*

2. ***Fans of Memoirs and Journals***

   - *People who enjoy raw, unfiltered, and personal accounts of someone's life journey, including challenges and triumphs, will connect with the narrative style.*

3. ***Advocates or Explorers of Psychedelics and Cannabis Culture***

   - *Readers interested in entheogens, their impact on creativity and thought processes, or experiences with substances like cannabis and magic mushrooms will relate to the detailed reflections.*

4. ***Travel Enthusiasts***

   - *The book references travel experiences and moments of serendipity in places like Jaisalmer and Ladakh, which might appeal to readers who enjoy stories of self-discovery through travel.*

5. ***Free Spirits and Non-Conformists***

   - *Individuals who resist societal norms, pursue alternative lifestyles, or question traditional measures of success may find resonance with the author's mindset.*

6. ***Fans of Unconventional Writing Styles***

- *The book's lack of rigid structure and conversational tone will attract readers who value experimental and organic storytelling over conventional formats.*

This book is likely to resonate most with open-minded and reflective individuals willing to engage with nuanced, experiential narratives.

[Questions 2 and 3 might seem like they have the same, or similar, answers despite the questions being worded differently. The questions were worded differently to check for the veracity, rigor, and robustness of ChatGPT's response. It's a good thing that the responses came out to be similar. It means ChatGPT does seem to know what it is talking about.]

PROLOGUE

By the way, the idea was to write this book after consuming entheogens – to see, and show, what my mind creates when on entheogens. I actually journalled the book all the way through under the influence.

It was this journalled book that I, first, wanted to publish. Midway through publication some events unfolded (story for another day) that made me decide not to publish the original journalled book like I really wanted to – and instead, rewrite the manuscript in a new form but with the core essence and stories intact.

As to why I took the decision I that I did, I will tell you someday if you really want to know (and if you do actually ask me about it). Sentimental reasons, actually.

My good friend – Axi, with whom I very recently struck a deep bond of friendship and to whom I had passed along the original version to read – really loved the original manuscript. He loved it so much especially because he got to get to know me – and more about me – through the original manuscript.

[At least, that is what he said to me]

In fact, now that I had decided not to publish the book in its original form, I wanted a version that was rewritten when I wasn't under any influence. As to why I wanted to do this is also a story for another day. And I promise to tell you about that too – but only if you really want to know and you actually do ask me about it.

It is this rewritten version – with Axi's (limited?) personal touch – that I finally decided to publish, and which you now read.

[By the way, if you want to know more about Axi, do read my other book – "Axi and Shashi: Volume 1". It will not only tell you how we came about but will also help you realize how that deep bond developed between us.]

There are some images that you will come across in this book. Some images will find immediate relevance in your mind when you go through the chapter(s). Some might seem irrelevant or confusing. If you give deeper thought to the text while observing the image closely, or vice versa, hopefully you will be able to sense or draw the connection that my mind drew between the text and the images. Maybe, you'd be able to see the philosophy in it too just as my mind did.

The images in this book are in black & white if you are reading a paperback. The reason for choosing a B/W version was to make it less expensive for you to purchase a hardcopy if you'd like to. If you want to see the 'colour version' of the book then I'd recommend you to download the eBook.

If you are reading the eBook, then the images will appear in colour anyway. But in case you want a laid-back read, and love the feel of a real book in your hand, I'd recommend the paperback (especially if you don't mind coming across B/W images).

[By the way, whatever answers and analysis by ChatGPT that you find in this book are all about the original manuscript – the one written while I was on entheogens. I decided to leave them in here anyway because this version of the book – the one where I rewrote it without being under any influence – has come out to be just as same with the core and essence and stories intact.]

If you'd like to see my absolute original manuscript in its raw, authentic, free-flowing form as is without any publication-ready edits – while under influence and without Axi's (limited) personal touch - then feel free to just reach out and ask for it. I will share with you a digital copy. Cost free.

[I actually, seriously, wish that you read both versions – this influence-free version and my original under-influence-manuscript version – so you can tell me which of those you liked/loved/preferred better (and why). So, I am hoping to hear from you directly about that if not about anything else.]

*****

This book, I hope, turns out not just an interesting and one-of-a-kind read for you but also becomes an experience for you someday .. [like it did for me]

INDEX

The Chapters – or 'Sessions' – in this book have no names and titles. The chapter name is whatever you decide and want it to be according to your perspective.

Every chapter is a session. Each session lasts for the duration of time I sat down to record my thoughts in one continuous sitting.

This book has 48 sessions - or 'chapters' - in total.

The idea, in my head, when I was writing this journal-cum-book was to keep it as continuous and as free flowing as possible.

The chapters - intentionally - have not been assigned any numbers in the titles and index during post-production pre-publishing basic editing. But this e-book has been split into separate numberless, title less sections digitally for easy access and navigation .. [or, as easy as possible access and navigation without compromising on the core essence of the journal]

Each chapter has the relevant chapter number either mentioned explicitly, or hidden somewhere, in it [except for one chapter mentioned in the index here]. The artistic - and logical - reason behind this decision is to let readers discover on their own which section corresponds to which chapter while going through the book in the hope that it offers them an experience as close as possible to the one that I had in mind while writing this journal and book.

When you reach chapter 30, you will see why.

Happy Reading!

DISCLAIMER

I have never smoked weed. I have never had cannabis in my system. I have never eaten magic mushrooms. I have never experimented with drugs or banned substances.

All stories and anecdotes in this book (if that's what you'd like to say this is) are completely made up. They never happened. If you come across any names or characters, they are all fake and figments of my imagination.

[Life is a dream after all, is it not?]

[That disclaimer was intended for the authorities and for the judicial system. Whether to believe it or not is entirely up to you – the reader. You can decide for yourself if this book is a work of fiction or not once you read it. Irrespective of whatever you choose to believe, I hope this book turns out to be a good read and you enjoy reading it just as much as I enjoyed writing it.]

CHAPTER

SESSION 01

For the love of law, liberty, freedom, and art, let's set the record straight—I do not smoke up. Now that we have that out of the way, let me take you on a journey through my musings, philosophy, stories, and the stray thoughts that find their way into my mind when it's set loose—floating freely, untethered, under the influence of something special.

I don't know if these words will ever find you. If you are reading them, then something in the universe aligned to make it happen. Maybe I found a publisher who didn't flinch at raw, unfiltered thoughts. Maybe I decided to let the world in on a part of me that usually stays hidden. I don't know what to call this collection of thoughts—book, journal, confession, experiment? That's for you to decide. If you must label it, do so for your own peace of mind. I simply write.

It's 18:40 in the evening, and I'm in Jaisalmer. A golden city bathed in the last light of the sun, ancient and whispering stories to those who know how to listen. My mind? A kite cut loose, drifting in the sky, carried by the winds of a 'special' cannabis cookie from the morning. And just for good measure, I had another bite before sitting down to write, nudging open the gates of deep thought and creative channeling.

Overcoming laziness to put words down is a battle of its own. Writing while high is an odd thing. Not because it isn't possible, but because when the mind takes flight, who wants to weigh it down with discipline? Structure? I find freedom in chaos. You may stumble upon repetition, because I don't reread what I write. These words flow as they come, like an open-ended conversation. If you stay long enough, patient enough, curious enough, maybe—just maybe—you'll begin to understand me a little better.

Cannabis has been my companion in these explorations, and magic mushrooms have been a willing guide. You'll see the why and how and what and when of it all as you move through these pages—if my words make sense to you. Or perhaps, if your own experiences have given you the ability to draw meaning from the madness. Who knows?

Entheogens shift perception in ways that are hard to describe. Time slows. The mind begins weaving intricate patterns between seemingly unrelated things. Dots that never connected before suddenly form constellations of thought. With good cannabis, the vibes are gentle, warm, expansive. With bad cannabis? Well, let's just say the mind can become a labyrinth with no exit.

Writing in this state requires a delicate balance—too lost in thought, and the words never make it to the page. Too structured, and the magic gets lost. So here I am, trying to capture the essence of what it means to think, to feel, to be, under the influence of something ancient, something sacred.

Today was a good day. The special cookie was delightful. So were the joints that followed. Perhaps that's why I finally overcame my inertia and set these thoughts down.

[Side note: I've been trying to convince my dear mother to try the cookies. She remains skeptical, hesitant. But who knows? Maybe someday curiosity will win.]

Before I go, a word of caution. Be wary of entheogens if you've been indulging for a while—even cannabis. There are things I've learned, the hard way, that I will share when the time feels right. It was a tricky, rocky road while it lasted. I wouldn't take it back, but I wouldn't recommend it lightly either.

That's enough for now. A good introduction. Time for a break. To be continued...

Mon, Jan 6

19:51

CHAPTER

Let me tell you a little about myself first. It always helps with perspective.

I was never the kind to work hard—at least, not until life demanded it. Or perhaps, demands it still.

My life turned out the way it did largely because of one undeniable stroke of fortune: I was born into a loving family. There was nothing extraordinary about it, no grand narrative of struggle or triumph, just the simple luck of growing up in a home where love was abundant.

I haven't worked a job in a while. Not because I couldn't, but because I didn't want to.

I tried the 9-to-5 routine once. It felt like I was suffocating inside a machine that wasn't built for me.

I tried entrepreneurship. The supposed dream of freedom and self-made success. But every time I chased an idea, I kept circling back to the same existential questions—"Why?" and "For whom?" I realized I wasn't building for myself. I wasn't even sure I wanted to build anything at all. So, I walked away.

Luckily, I didn't have to stay in the race. My grandfather left behind enough of an inheritance that, with a little wisdom in investing, could sustain me for the rest of my life. Food, shelter, and time—three things I realized were more valuable than any paycheck. That gave me the freedom to step away, to stop running, and to start truly living on my own terms.

There was a time when I worked hard just to prove something—to myself, to others. I wanted to be seen, validated, acknowledged. But that was a younger, more restless version of me, one who hadn't yet learned that self-worth isn't found in external approval. Life, with its lessons and bruises, has a way of making you wiser.

Teaching was my passion for a while. I stood in classrooms, shared knowledge, and in return, learned more from my students than I ever expected. It made me fall in love with the art of teaching. But like most things, life shifted, and that chapter became a memory rather than a path forward.

Now, writing suits me better.

I can write at my own pace, in my own time, from wherever I want. No deadlines.

No obligations. Just me, my thoughts, and the slow unfolding of my mind onto paper.

Like many before me, I have wandered through life searching for purpose. The search never really ends. Purpose morphs as you grow, adapting to the different stages of your life. The need for purpose never goes away, but the shape of it does.

Perhaps, in this moment, my purpose is to document. To put down in words the experiences, musings, and lessons that life has gifted me. Not for personal gain.

Not to teach or preach. But simply as an example of how a life—my life—has unfolded.

I share these thoughts with you not because I must, but because I want to.

I have been having conversations with you in my mind for years. This is the first time I'm recording them.

I write when I feel like it. Am I good at it? I don't know. I don't particularly care. Art is subjective. Beauty and mediocrity are just perspectives. Everything is relative.

A good friend nudged me recently—encouraged me to share. And so, I thought, why not? Maybe one day, Maggie, my little sweetheart of a niece, will stumble upon these musings and get to know me in ways she never had the chance to before. Maybe, through these words, she'll understand how I saw life. Who knows?

Right now, I'm sitting next to a temple inside a living fort, the scent of old stones and incense mixing with the cool winter air. The cannabis in my system settles me into a deep stillness. If I could, I'd tell you all about the people I've met, the stories they've carried, the strange, wonderful moments I've had under the influence of entheogens. But I can't. Not in detail, anyway. Privacy. Legalities. Sentiments.

What I can do is share the lessons they've left me with—the philosophies, the insights. And most of those have come to me when I've been high. Usually on cannabis. It's reliable, gentle, familiar. It has gifted me experiences unlike anything else. Magic mushrooms, too, but they're not as easy to come by.

My mother disapproves of all of it.

She worries. Of course, she does. That's what loving mothers do. She sees cannabis as dangerous. And yet, she knows I use it sometimes. I've never hidden it from her. Never needed to. Never wanted to. Over time, she has come to accept me as I am, just as I have come to accept her for who she is. We don't always agree, but the love remains, unchanged.

She was sitting right next to me earlier today—technically, I was sitting next to her—when I wrote the first chapter. She had no idea what I was writing. Not that it would have mattered.

I wonder if she'll ever read this book.

I haven't told anyone I'm writing it. Not yet. I'd rather let it exist quietly, let it be discovered naturally. There's something poetic about that. Time will tell.

Jaisalmer has been good to me. The winter breeze, the sandstone streets, the golden light of the fort—it's all worked its way into my soul. This trip has been like a clearing of the mind, sweeping away dilemmas and leaving behind clarity.

New people, same humanity. Same people, new perspectives.

So many existential questions have been answered by the universe, effortlessly, as if they were always waiting for me to ask the right way.

That's what cannabis does to me. It slows time, stitches connections between thoughts, opens doors in the mind that I didn't even know were there. It fuels my art. My words. My laughter.

And today, there was a lot of laughter.

Happy times. Good vibes.

Weed effect.

21:07

End of Chapter 2.

CHAPTER

2025

What a year to be alive.

Not for the usual reasons people throw around—technological advancements, political shifts, cultural evolutions—but for the number itself. Mathematically, 2025 is fascinating. It holds certain properties, certain patterns that make it stand out. There's something poetic about numbers, how they carry hidden meanings, quietly waiting for those who know where to look.

I have always been drawn to thinking—*really* thinking. Not just idle daydreams or fleeting curiosities, but deep contemplation about anything that captures my attention and refuses to let go. It has been both a blessing and a curse.

Some thoughts expand the mind, spark insight, and offer clarity. Others loop endlessly, spiraling into questions with no answers, shadows without form. Whether this trait is a strength or a flaw depends entirely on the situation. Context is everything. What is good in one moment can be bad in another. What is clarity to one person might be chaos to another.

And speaking of context—that is what makes storytelling so difficult.

A story is never just a sequence of events. It is a mosaic of details, personalities, emotions, and timing. Stripped of its context, a story loses something vital. You can still tell it, yes, but it won't breathe the same way. It won't carry the same weight. Without knowing the people involved, without understanding who they were in that exact moment in time, the essence of the story dissolves.

That is why I hesitate.

There are things I want to tell you, stories I want to share. Some are simple. Some are anything but. And yet, I find myself caught between the desire to lay it all out and the understanding that words alone may not be enough.

Still, I am not one to shy away from a challenge.

Perhaps, with time, I will find a way. A way to tell you as much as I can without losing what matters. A way to preserve the essence of these stories, even if I cannot give you every single thread of the tapestry.

Let's see. Time has a way of revealing possibilities we cannot yet imagine.

End of Chapter 3.

CHAPTER

CHAPTER 4

It's a good morning.

The kind of morning where the mind feels light, the air feels crisp, and the world seems to be in no rush to demand anything from you. Last night, we shared a drink—barely half a bottle of coffee rum between five people. Just enough for a warm buzz, not enough to make the night slip into a blur. Of course, there was some weed too. The laughter was effortless, contagious, unfiltered.

Alcohol erases time, makes the edges of memory soft and malleable. But cannabis—cannabis is different. It doesn't just let you remember; it keeps your mind sharp enough that there is no forgetting to begin with. Everything stays. Every joke, every tangent of thought, every little epiphany that would have otherwise been lost in the noise of the world. I think, after years of trial and error,

I've found the perfect balance. Or maybe I just think I have. Who knows?

One habit I wish I hadn't picked up in the last couple of years is smoking tobacco.

It's time to let it go—I can feel it. It's not doing much for me anymore. It's not a *bad* habit, not in the grand scheme of things, but it's also not a *good* one. Unlike cannabis, it doesn't take my mind anywhere new. No heightened awareness, no creative spark—just something to do when thinking. A placeholder.

I feel it in my breathing now, that subtle heaviness when I exert myself too much. Is it age creeping in? Or is it just the smoking? I suspect the latter. And I appreciate the people around me who remind me that I've been smoking more than I should. These are the small, natural alarms that society builds into itself.

The question is—will I listen?

I'd like to think so.

After all, if I'm aware enough to write about it, then maybe I'm wise enough to stop when the time is right. Time will tell.

For those wondering—I don't do cannabis often. Only when traveling, only where it's accessible (legally, ideally), and only when I truly *want* to. I use it to think—*really* think. To let my mind stretch its legs and wander down paths I might not explore otherwise. Sometimes, it's just for an evening of good company, authentic conversations, and laughter that comes from the gut.

But here's the thing—I have learned that cannabis is best enjoyed in moderation.

A while ago, I had so much of it in my system that it triggered something in me.

Psychosis, they called it. I have my own theories. Maybe one day, I'll tell you what I did during that phase. It's funny, looking back now. But at the time? It was chaos, not just for me, but for some others as well.

Quality matters.

Organic, natural, untampered cannabis? That's the good stuff. Euphoria, warmth, clarity. You feel connected to yourself, to your thoughts, to the universe. But the hybrid, chemically altered strains? They left me feeling *stoned* rather than *high*. There's a difference. A big one. And anything contaminated with chemical additives—best avoided. They don't just dull the mind; they twist it, warp reality in ways that aren't always easy to come back from.

A *good* high is when thoughts flow like water, when ideas link together seamlessly, when your mind takes you places you didn't even realize you needed to go. It's when you see connections you had never noticed before—between memories, emotions, experiences. It's when life itself starts to make a little more sense. Not just your life, but the entire *universe*.

I wish I had a way with words to capture it all exactly as it feels.

My vocabulary isn't what it used to be. I don't reach for complex words anymore. My writing has become simpler, more natural. Maybe that's just how it is now. Maybe that will change again.

This morning, the urge to write came naturally. I rolled out of bed, smoked a couple of bidis—just tobacco—and burrowed under the blanket with my phone. It's easier this way, typing instead of writing by hand. Laziness, maybe. Efficiency, definitely.

Halfway through, I stepped outside, shared a joint with friends, and let the morning sunlight wash over me.

That's when the thoughts started hitting in waves.

It's frustrating sometimes, the way thoughts come and go. There's no machine that can capture them exactly as they are, no device that can extract the mind's raw stream of consciousness and put it into words. I wish there was. Maybe someday, someone will invent it. Maybe someday, it will be possible to take even the most abstract thought and break it down into something measurable, understandable, tangible.

But for now, all we have is language. And language, as beautiful as it is, is never perfect.

Time itself is relative—but so is the perception of time.

A decade means nothing to a 50-year-old. It's just 20% of his life, a fraction of his experience. But for a 10-year-old? A decade is *everything*. It is his entire world, his entire existence. Same amount of time—completely different weight.

See what I mean?

It's never just *what* you think. It's always *how* you think it.

No?

End of Chapter 4.

CHAPTER

Chapter 4 ended a while ago.

This is the fifth.

I don't know what kind of structure this book will take, if it will follow any conventional order or if it even needs one. Right now, it feels more like a collection of *sittings* than actual *chapters*—each piece written in a single stretch, capturing thoughts as they come, unfiltered, unstructured, raw. Maybe that's how it's meant to be. Maybe this book isn't about structure at all, but about moments.

When cannabis lifts you—when your mind takes flight and drifts effortlessly from one thought to another—it's like being unshackled. No rigid pathways, no imposed directions, just free flow. That's always been one of the things I love most about it.

And setting matters.

Not that writing *requires* the perfect setting, but it shapes the experience. The weather, the food, the view—all of it adds to the mood, the *vibe*. A quiet place, an open sky, the right kind of breeze, and suddenly, thoughts feel clearer, deeper, more alive. Right now, I'm sitting on a peaceful terrace, watching the world move at its own rhythm. There's something about this moment—the stillness, the openness, the silence that isn't really silent.

I often find myself locked in deep philosophical conversations—with myself, mostly. The right entheogen in my system makes those conversations richer, fuller, more immersive. I think about sharing them as they happen, about capturing them in their purest form. But the moment always feels so vast, so layered, that by the time I sit down to write, it's already faded into something smaller. Writing about it later feels like painting a landscape from memory—some details remain, but the essence is harder to grasp. What I end up with is just the *gist* of it.

Still, I try.

Have you ever read the news while high? If you haven't, I'd recommend it. Not for the content itself, but for the perspective shift it brings. The way the words unfold, the way patterns emerge, the way hidden undercurrents become more visible. It's like peeling back a layer of reality you never realized was there. Personally, I love doing it sometimes. It makes the world feel both absurd and perfectly understandable at the same time.

I take more time to open up now.

There was a time when it came easily, naturally, without hesitation. Somewhere along the way, I changed. Not in a bad way, just... evolved. The journey from *there* to *here* has been full of lessons—some hard, some beautiful, some I'm still making sense of. There have been downs, yes. But there have been good *ups* too.

These days, when I do open up, it's usually through writing.

And maybe, for now, that's enough.

CHAPTER

CHAPTER 6

[So, to continue...]

Life has been a strange journey for me.

But then again, isn't it strange for all of us?

Experience, as they say, is the best teacher. It took me a long time to truly understand what that meant—not just intellectually, but viscerally. You can read about something a hundred times, hear countless people talk about it, analyze it from a distance, but until it happens to *you*, it remains just an idea.

Emotional turmoil was one of those things for me.

I always *knew* what it was. I had seen it in others, read about it, watched it unfold in stories and movies. I thought I understood it. But understanding something from the outside is one thing—feeling it is something else entirely. When it finally found me, it wasn't just a passing experience; it was a force. It shattered, reshaped, and remolded me. It became a teacher in ways no book, no conversation, no abstract contemplation ever could.

It forced me to confront truths about myself—some light, some dark, some I wasn't ready for. It peeled back layers I didn't even know existed.

One of those truths had been sitting quietly inside me since childhood, but over the last decade and a half, it became undeniable: *I am not meant for marriage.*

I had sensed it early on, but experience carved it into conviction. It's not that I see marriage as something inherently bad. I understand why people seek it, why they find comfort in it, why it becomes a central pillar of their lives. But for me? The very thought feels like a cage.

It's not about commitment. It's about *freedom*.

The idea of losing my independence, of being bound by expectations and responsibilities that don't align with who I am, unsettles me deeply. I have watched too many people lose themselves in the name of companionship—compromising their essence, dulling their edges to fit into a mold, sacrificing parts of themselves they once held sacred.

I don't want that.

As I write this to you, I wonder—will I ever change my mind? Life has a way of throwing unexpected twists our way. But at this moment, in this chapter of my existence, I feel certain. My path is meant to be walked alone, not out of loneliness, but out of choice.

And there's a quiet kind of peace in that.

CHAPTER 7

Sorry for starting the seventh so abruptly.

I was deep into writing the sixth when a friend dropped by, pulling me into the currents of life. The moment shifted, the flow changed, and whatever I had meant to tell you slipped away—just like that. It's strange how thoughts, no matter how vivid or urgent they feel in one moment, can dissolve into nothingness when interrupted by the real world.

But then, isn't that the nature of existence?

Tonight, without any pre-planning—just the universe unfolding as it does—I decided to test my limits a little. No grand intentions, no careful calculations. Just the last night with friends before everyone disperses in their own directions. A special cookie found its way to me. Medium strength. Paired it with some CoffeeRum. Just happened.

[As usual, a story for another day.]

It had been a good day. One of those days where life surprises you in the gentlest ways. I heard from friends I had thought were long gone, lost to time and distance. But somehow, they circled back. Life has a way of doing that—bringing people together in ways you never see coming. Beautiful coincidences. Or maybe nothing is ever truly a coincidence.

So far, I feel steady. Balanced. I am present, aware, fully in control of my mind, which is always the key when experimenting with altered states. It's a comforting realization—to know your limits without losing yourself. A fine line, but an important one.

I've stepped away from the "party" for a while, just to record this moment, to document the vibe before it drifts away. The night is alive, the air carries laughter, and the energy around me is warm and light. It's one of those rare instances where everything feels aligned—like the universe itself is at ease.

I will likely go back in soon, but I know I've had enough for tonight. No more additions to the mix. It's a strange thing, moderation. One needs to know when to stop, when to step back, when to let the moment breathe without pushing it further.

Right now, I am at an organic farm cum hotel with some friends. The food is good. The company is easy. The stars above feel closer than usual.

And in this moment, all is well.

About three years ago—2022—I found myself in a mental observation facility.

It wasn't something I had planned, nor was I even aware of where I was being taken. One moment, I was in the familiar world of my own mind, and the next, I was being whisked away to a place where people would watch, analyze, and attempt to categorize the contents of that very mind. My sister had arranged for it.

The official diagnosis? Cannabis Dependent Schizoaffective Disorder—SAD, ironically enough. SAD is something that strikes you and then goes away on its own – naturally.

Some doctors disagreed. They thought it was Bipolar Affective Disorder (BAPD). Another was convinced it was Schizophrenia. That last one didn't sit well with me. Schizophrenia? That required proof. So, I conducted an experiment—a daring, deliberate exercise in logic and self-awareness—to show them otherwise. Ten days later, I had made my case. Schizophrenia was ruled out.

I spent eight weeks under observation.

By the way, SAD is given as a diagnosis when a patient shows some (not all, or most) signs of Schizophrenia and some of BAPD but doesn't fit into the criteria of either. I still haven't told you about doctors who thought everything was okay with me and the incidents in my life were simple cannabis-triggered-psychosis episodes with justifiable paranoia given the activism and career field I was focused on. Also, more stories about my "THC" stay later in future volumes, if they happen at all.

For most patients, the diagnostic process takes two or three weeks. Mine took longer. The doctors restarted their analysis multiple times, unable to settle on a single, definite conclusion. I had to repeat my experiment—this time, to confirm my own observations. When I finally understood what was happening, I made my one permitted phone call per week—to my sister. Not just because she was the one who put me there, but because she needed to hear what I had uncovered.

Eventually, she was convinced.

"I think you're okay enough to come home."

That statement alone was enough to get me out of there. Against medical advice, she signed me out. The next two weeks, I stayed at her place. She wanted to be sure—wanted to see for herself if what I had told her was real, or if I had simply learned to play the system. My niece was there too—oblivious, innocent, as a child should be. To her, it was just another visit from her uncle.

2022 was not an isolated event.

It was the culmination of something that had started around 2016. Back then, I was deeply immersed in political activism, studying law, forming strong opinions, and voicing them openly on social media. At the same time, smoking locally available Cannabis had become part of my daily life—part student life, part rebellion, part exploration.

I knew cannabis could cause short-term paranoia and anxiety. What I didn't know back then was that long-term effects were possible too. THC lingers in the system, stored in fat cells, releasing slowly over time. The science wasn't widely documented. Cannabis had been classified as a banned narcotic—not because its effects were fully understood, but because they weren't.

And in my case, paranoia took root.

Government surveillance. Secret Service operations. Hidden hands pulling unseen strings. I wasn't just thinking about these things—I was feeling them, living them. I was convinced that power was being abused, that I was being watched. And I acted on those fears.

As an activist, a law student, and a believer in justice, I was no stranger to stories of governments silencing voices. And my own life seemed to be running in parallel with these stories—strange coincidences, unexplainable events, patterns I couldn't ignore. So, I pushed back. Digitally. Publicly. Unapologetically.

It was thrilling.

It was reckless.

And it was all done without malice. My heart was in the right place, even if my logic had been skewed. I never felt guilty for what I did—only for the collateral damage it caused. Some people got caught in the whirlwind, if only temporarily, and for that, I am sorry. When I eventually realized that my actions had been driven more by paranoia and overthinking than by reality, regret set in.

But then, at THC—The Healing Center (ironically, the name of the mental observation facility my sister had me committed to)—I learned something else.

It wasn't just me.

It was Cannabis—or rather, what Cannabis had become.

Pure, natural, unadulterated Cannabis had never done this to me before. But the Cannabis I had been smoking in Delhi was different. Adulterated. Laced with chemicals. Peddlers often mix substances to amplify effects, to create a heavier, more intoxicating high. And that is what pushed me beyond the edge. That is what blurred the lines between rational thought and irrational suspicion.

It was a harsh lesson—one that showed me what entheogens can do when taken carelessly, without proper precautions.

And this wasn't the first time something like this had happened.

Back in 2018, I had a similar episode. A quieter one. My uncle—concerned but discreet—took me to see a psychiatrist. No explanations, no warnings. Just a request to take a few prescribed pills for a week. I complied. But curiosity got the better of me. I researched the medication and found out they were antipsychotics—used for Schizophrenia.

That confused me.

Schizophrenia? That diagnosis didn't match my symptoms at all.

I dismissed the whole thing as a misdiagnosis by an incompetent shrink and moved on. Life returned to normal. Or so I thought.

But now, looking back, I question everything.

How much of what happened was real? How much was misunderstood? The diagnoses at THC felt inconsistent, rushed, almost forced. The third and final one seemed like a last-ditch attempt to keep me under observation longer. But the moment I stopped consuming that adulterated Cannabis, everything became clear. My mind steadied. Since then, I have smoked natural Cannabis several times, and never once have I experienced the same paranoia or instability.

So, were the doctors wrong? Or am I just unwilling to accept that they might have been right?

I don't know.

But I do know this: I have moderated my Cannabis use significantly since then. Not because I regret it. Not because I fear it. But because, on the off chance that even one of those doctors was right, I am willing to be cautious.

Funny, shocking, and unbelievable things happened during that time. Stories I could fill an entire book with. Maybe I will someday. Maybe Cannabis lovers need to hear this as part of their knowledge base—not to scare them, but to inform them. To give them a tale of caution. A documented mental and neural experiment. A guide on what to do and what not to do.

You get the gist, right?

But let me be clear—I do not regret any of it.

My mind may have wandered, but what it brought back with it—the reflections, memories, learnings, and philosophies—are priceless. Had it not been for Cannabis, I would not have seen what I saw. I would not have learned what I learned.

Some people gain wisdom through life experiences, through relationships, emotions, and everyday attachments.

Some find it through meditation, introspection, and reflection.

And then, some—like me—choose to explore through entheogens.

I do it not just to see how it affects my brain and perspective, but because it accelerates deep philosophical, spiritual, and scientific thinking. It fast-tracks wisdom in a way that experience alone cannot. No one can live through all possible scenarios in a single lifetime. But entheogens? They offer glimpses.

That is why I choose this path.

But this is my path.

Not yours.

Not anyone else's.

What works for me may not work for you. What unlocks something in me may not do the same for you. If you seek wisdom, find your own way. Whether through experience, meditation, or psychedelics—let it be your choice.

The path is yours to walk.

[End of Day's Play and Chapter 8]

CHAPTER

I just reread a part of Chapter 8. Something felt missing. So, I added some context. Not my usual style—going back and editing my own words after they've already been written—but here we are.

Feels a bit like cheating, honestly. Like I told you a story, and before you could truly hear it, I slipped in a few more details, adjusted the lighting, and changed the angles. But maybe that's just how memory works anyway—constantly reshaping itself, adding layers, polishing over the rough spots, making sense of what once felt like chaos.

I've always loved the intellectual stimulation that cannabis brings me. The way it turns the ordinary into something worth dissecting. The way it makes conversations spiral into the profound, the ridiculous, and the beautifully absurd all at once. But my most transformative entheogenic experience? That title belongs to *Magic Mushrooms*.

2012.

Kodaikanal.

That was the moment my perspective on life shifted—not subtly, not gently, but like an earthquake cracking the very foundation of my thoughts. I *felt* things

I had never felt before. *Saw* things I could never unsee. Understood truths that, once revealed, felt so obvious that I couldn't fathom how I had lived without them. That trip was so powerful, so life-altering, that I even brought some shrooms back home for my mother. I wanted her to experience it, to see the world through the lens that had opened up before me.

One day, if our conversation leads to it, I'll tell you about that trip in detail. Some things deserve their own time, their own space to be told properly.

For now, I sit here in Jaisalmer, music playing softly in the background—*The Godfather Love Theme* drifting through the air from Spotify. The golden city stands still outside my window, ancient and unmoved by the restless minds of travelers passing through. And yet, my own thoughts wander, stretching back across the years, across the places I have been, the people I have known.

Some people miss out on money. Some miss out on love. Some miss out on time. Some miss experiences.

I miss the endless intellectual banter. The late-night debates that start with something trivial and spiral into the meaning of existence. The shared laughter that echoes long after the moment is gone. I miss people, too. The ones who were once so close. The ones who brought good vibes, good times. The ones who are now just names in my phone that I rarely press call on.

This trip to Jaisalmer has been good to me. It sorted things out in my head—made the intangible a little more tangible. I met beautiful souls, had conversations that left imprints on my mind, tripped harmlessly on good *bhang* and *ganja*. Reunited with friends. Even had a few of life's lingering existential questions answered.

Half a year ago, my trip to Ladakh was serendipitous. I wasn't looking for anything in particular, but I found something anyway—solo souls wandering the same path, people who were strangers one moment and closer than lifelong friends the next. Those kinds of connections don't happen often, but when they do, they carve out a place in you forever. That trip left me with a suitcase full of stories—some of which I'll tell, some of which I'll keep just for myself.

Right now, life feels... peaceful. More than it has in a long time.

For an atheist like me, even I was surprised when I found myself stepping into a temple here and praying. My mother, even more so. She watched me with quiet astonishment, not quite knowing what to make of it. But some places, some moments, just stir something in you. And I think this trip, this journey—of Jaisalmer, of Ladakh, of traveling with her—has been about something more than just seeing new places.

She has spent her whole life *giving*. Every ounce of herself. Never once pausing to take. This is my way of giving something back, my way of nudging her into embracing life for herself now. I want her to move beyond the confines of being a tourist, to step into the world as a traveler, to feel the thrill of discovery instead of just checking off sights from a list.

So far, we've only been to Ladakh and Jaisalmer together. But there will be more.

Family vacations from childhood don't count. Those were different. Those were orchestrated, structured, planned down to the last meal. This… this is different.

Got to go now—friends just walked in with food from a nearby restaurant. Smells amazing. Catch you later.

For now, let's call this *The End of Chapter 9.*

CHAPTER

CHAPTER 10

January 9, 2025.

Woke up at 4:30 AM today. The kind of wakefulness that feels abrupt, like something within already knew it was time. Time to say goodbye. Time to let go again.

A couple of friends are leaving, bags packed, tickets confirmed, heading back to wherever life has placed them. I stood there, exchanged a few words, a few nods, a few lingering glances that carried more than words ever could.

No clue when life will bring us together again. If it ever will. Time does what it wants. We think we have control, that we make plans, but in the end, it's always time that decides. Only time can tell.

Twenty minutes now. A stretch of quiet solitude between goodbyes and whatever comes next. A small window for essentials—brushing off the remnants of sleep, sipping water, stretching limbs stiff from the night. And contemplation, of course. There's always room for that.

I think they're still asleep. Or at least, they were when I last checked. Maybe I'll steal a few more minutes of sleep myself before the final farewells. Drift back under the warm weight of my blanket, let the winter air outside exist without me for a little while longer.

It's chilly. The kind of cold that makes you second-guess leaving your cocoon. The kind that whispers, *Stay. Just a little more.*

The blanket is tempting. Too tempting.

CHAPTER

CHAPTER 11

6:49 AM

Bid adieu to friends. Another set of goodbyes, another reminder that life never stops moving.

I used to find farewells difficult. There was always a lingering ache, a reluctance to let go. But as I grow older, I realize that sentiments fade while philosophy takes the wheel. Attachments that once felt like anchors are now more like passing waves—touching, shifting, then rolling away. I don't hold on as tightly anymore.

One thing I have come to accept in life: if the universe wills it, it will happen. If our paths are meant to cross again, they will. If not, then perhaps they were never meant to.

Speaking of the universe, I had planned to rent a ride today and take Mother deeper into the desert—far beyond the usual tourist paths, into the stillness where sand and sky stretch endlessly. There were places I had in mind, places I wanted her to see.

But I leave it up to fate. If she wakes before 9, we go. If not, we don't. No expectations, no forcing plans. Today is our last day in Jaisalmer—this trip, at least.

I often tell young people not to rush into Cannabis, especially before 25. Not because of some rigid scientific argument, but because I believe the human mind needs time to fully mature—not just in logic and reason but in emotion, in resilience.

Puberty is already a storm. A flood of change, confusion, and self-discovery. The early years of adulthood should be about living life raw, unfiltered—without substances that distort perception, no matter how enlightening they may be. Travel, relationships, heartbreak, friendships, failures—these experiences should shape you first. Entheogens like Cannabis help you *process* life, but first, you must have lived enough of it to process.

Cannabis is often labeled an "ambition killer." I once believed that too. There was a time when I thought I had lost my drive to succeed—both professionally and academically.

When I was running my second venture, I hit an existential wall. The deeper I looked into myself, the more I questioned *why* I was even doing it. The endless chase for success, the pressure to build, to achieve, to prove something—it all felt hollow.

I stopped when I found my answer.

But Cannabis, as I later realized, was never the *killer* of ambition. It was a filter, a revealer. The ones who call it an ambition killer are often those who misunderstand it.

Whether I was always this philosophical, this introspective—or whether Cannabis brought it out in me—I don't know. What I *do* know is that Cannabis became a gift in my life. A tool that pulled back the curtain and made me see things as they truly were.

I didn't *lose* ambition. I *outgrew* it. It transformed into something deeper, something more meaningful. The 'whys' and 'hows' of my actions became clearer. The so-called 'rat race' wasn't for me—not because I couldn't run it, but because I saw no real *point* in it.

Cannabis, to some extent, led me toward a new path. My definition of ambition changed. Instead of chasing conventional success, I sought something else entirely—the ability to spend my time doing what I love, without harming or burdening anyone.

I saw how, in my younger years, I had sometimes pursued things for *validation*—to be seen, to be acknowledged, to be considered 'successful' by society's standards. But my older self? He doesn't care for that. He seeks inner peace, self-awareness, and freedom.

Cannabis did not kill my ambition. It refined it. It stripped away the illusions and left behind only what truly mattered.

I didn't quit jobs or walk away from ventures because Cannabis drained my ambition. I did it because I saw how *needless* so many responsibilities were. How *rigid* and *suffocating* societal expectations could be. I did it because I understood how empty the chase was.

I chose something else. A quiet life. A free life. One where I could travel, think, grow, evolve—without the weight of meaningless obligations pressing down on me.

This won't happen to everyone. But it happened to me.

And for that, I find myself thanking the universe.

7:39 AM

CHAPTER

CHAPTER 12

My journey with entheogens didn't begin in youthful recklessness. It wasn't the thrill of rebellion or the pressure of peers that led me down that path. It was a conscious choice—one I made only after turning 25.

It's not that I hadn't encountered the opportunity earlier. The world around me had always been full of offerings—temptations, curiosities, invitations. But when I was younger, a promise held me back.

My father and I had once spoken about my (then future) hostel life. In that conversation, he made me promise something simple yet profound: *No bad habits until you graduate. Until you are truly independent.*

At the time, I agreed without much thought. It seemed reasonable. Besides, hostel life itself was more exciting than any distractions it could offer.

Fate, however, had other plans.

Not long after that conversation, I lost my father in a car accident. The weight of his absence turned that promise into something sacred. It was no longer just a casual agreement—it was a vow, a connection to him that I wasn't willing to break.

And so, I kept it.

The first time I partied with entheogens was the day I graduated. A quiet sense of completion settled over me. I had upheld my word. Now, it was time to step into a new phase—on my terms.

That night, I drank alcohol for the first time. Rum, if I remember correctly. And I tried Cannabis—not as an edible, but smoked.

Not that I hadn't sampled other things before.

At 18, I had my first puff of tobacco—a Marlboro. The moment was unplanned. I was in Mysore for my Air Force SSB (Service Selection Board) interview. Our Officer-in-Command, while showing us candidate cadets around, casually offered me a cigarette.

"Try," he said. *"See what happens. Feel what it's like."*

I did. Two puffs. Nothing more.

Alcohol came into my life much later. I was 22, traveling to Thailand. On the flight, a stewardess poured a glass of wine in front of me.

"Just one sip," encouraged an uncle sitting beside me, nudging me toward the experience with a knowing smile.

I took the sip. Just enough to know what alcohol really was.

Cannabis, too, entered my life at 22. Hostel life in Pune. A friend introduced it to me.

Two puffs. That's all.

Unlike most, I had never grown up fearing Cannabis. I had seen people smoke in front of me, but I had never witnessed madness or chaos. There were no stories of people losing their minds, no erratic behavior, no violent outbursts.

If anything, the experience was always the opposite. Conversations turned profound, humorous, and strangely insightful. Some of my friends swore by it—not just as an escape, but as a means to tap into a different layer of thought.

And so, my dorm room in Pune became a sanctuary. A haven for those who found solace in the slow-burning wisdom of Cannabis.

It was ironic, really. Society demonized it, labeled it dangerous, even illegal. In India, it was still classified as a banned narcotic. To most families, getting caught with it would be disgraceful.

But inside that small room, none of that mattered.

It wasn't a den of addicts—it was a refuge for thinkers, seekers, and souls wanting to connect.

[Out with Mum for some food. Sampling something new here. The dishes have arrived. Our conversation shall continue.]

CHAPTER

I turned 40 last December.

Strange how time moves. When I think of being 25, or even 18, it feels like a lifetime ago. Yet, in certain moments, it all feels like yesterday—as if I could blink and find myself back there.

Like most young people, I once equated age with wisdom, assuming that the older one got, the more they *knew.* But life has a way of unraveling such naive assumptions.

It isn't age that makes one wise. It is experience.

And experience is unpredictable. Sometimes, you live a single moment stretched across lifetimes. Other times, lifetimes collapse into a single, fleeting moment.

Has that ever happened to you?

It has to me.

And for that, I am grateful.

Fifteen years of intermittent entheogenic experiments do not make me a scholar of the field, let alone a guru. But it is still something. More than many, perhaps. Less than some. Enough to have learned a thing or two.

As I write this, I hope I will continue documenting life and its experiences—especially the entheogenic ones—as much as possible, for as long as I can.

Maybe, for someone out there, these words will serve as a map to trace the long-term effects of my entheogenic journeys. Maybe, when my books or writings are read start to finish, a pattern will emerge—something more revealing than I could ever consciously articulate.

Or maybe not. Maybe none of this will matter.

If you've followed my story this far, you have probably realized that my life is neither exceptional nor remarkable.

I am not a gifted writer. My vocabulary is simple. Not because I don't understand complex literature, but because I rarely commit words to memory. Why bother when everything is searchable? It's the age of Google, after all.

But I *was* born in an interesting time—1984, the *Orwellian Dystopia.*

When I was three, televisions were becoming household staples, and landlines were still a novelty. The world was shifting, though we had no idea just how much.

Now, I look ahead. The next milestone—42. The magic number. *Thank you, Douglas Adams.*

If you want to know more about how my life played out, it's out there—on LinkedIn, for now. Though, who knows? Maybe LinkedIn itself will disappear someday. Maybe my profile will be lost to the digital void. If the universe truly wants you to find it, you will. And if not, then perhaps it's better left unknown.

Much of what I have done, tried, and lived feels incidental anyway. Sometimes, the journey is immaterial if the destination is worth it.

I suppose I should tell you why my startups shut down.

The first one? Arguments between co-founders on how to run it. I think I was pushed out, though maybe that was just a convenient excuse. In the end, it didn't matter. I wasn't willing to compromise on certain principles. I wasn't willing to change my way of working just to fit in. And when you *know,* you *know.*

Still, it was hard. That was also the time when a breakup hit me like a wrecking ball. Looking back, I could have handled it better, but I didn't. Instead, I found myself dissecting my own weaknesses, insecurities, and desires—those deep, hidden layers of self that only emerge when life forces you to confront them.

The second startup? I shut it down myself.

Remember that THC experience I mentioned earlier? That's when it all unfolded.

Something about that time—*those* events, *those* experiences—made me realize what I truly *did not* want to do. Managing and building a *business* wasn't for me. Working a job somewhere? Definitely not.

It had always been about something else: Bringing new ideas to life. Leaving behind something meaningful. Building a small fund—just enough for a modest life, to travel freely without grand expectations.

The ideas I had? Someone, somewhere, would bring them to life eventually. Science and innovation march forward with or without us.

Leaving behind an *inspirational* legacy? For whom? And why?

I'd rather leave behind an *honest* one. A documented record, unpolished and real.

Inspiration is subjective, after all.

I was a fairly decent teacher for a while. Not as great as I wished to be, but not terrible either.

Some of my students became close friends. But then came 2022. The THC incident. The brief two-month 'imprisonment.'

I became a nuisance to some, burned bridges, lost old friendships—some of them beautiful, some irreplaceable.

Maybe, one day, those who were affected by that time will understand what was truly happening. Maybe our bonds will be restored. Maybe not.

Who knows?

Only the universe.

(Perhaps they'll read this book out of curiosity, just like you are now.)

As I write this, I have consumed a special cookie—moderate strength—and washed it down with a *super* strong *bhang thandai.*

So far, my mind and body handle it well. There's a mild buzz, a clear stream of thoughts, a sense of depth and acknowledgment.

No laughter today, just occasional smiles as memories surface. A peaceful, pensive solitude.

Friends left early this morning. I will leave tomorrow. But for now, I savor the quiet, the city, the fort. It feels as though the universe intended me to be here in this moment.

(By the way, if you ever find yourself too high on bhang or Cannabis, just drink 1–2 glasses of lemonade. No sugar. Worked for me. It brings the high down safely and smoothly.)

I just heard an incredible story.

A friend of a friend, an artist who also cooks here in Jaisalmer. Apparently, the best pizza he ever made was under the influence of an entheogen.

If only you were here to hear it firsthand.

But for now, I head out.

One last goodbye to some new friends.

CHAPTER

CHAPTER 14

January 10, 2025 – 01:34 AM

Some days etch themselves into memory with a peculiar clarity, as if the universe itself conspires to make them stand out. Today was one of those days.

Jaisalmer—this golden city of sand and stone—had already gifted me more than I had expected. But tonight, in the lingering haze of cannabis and conversation, something clicked. A thought. An idea. One of those rare ones that feel like they're meant to be pursued. The kind that buzzes in your mind long after the high has faded.

The extra dose of cannabis helped, I won't deny it. So did the lingering warmth of an evening well spent, exchanging stories with strangers who no longer felt like strangers. A little alcohol swirled in my system too, adding its own quiet hum to the mix.

And then the thought arrived—simple, yet profound.

Imagine an open invitation. A journey. A gift.

Flights covered. Stay covered. Food and internal travel left to the traveler. Ten days. No expectations, no rules, no itinerary. Come as you are. Leave when you want. Just bring your curiosity, your willingness to wander. A space for solo travelers to find themselves in the echoes of new landscapes, in the kindness of fleeting friendships, in the stories that unfold when the familiar is left behind.

I know what travel can do to a person. My first visit to Sikkim back in 2010 was the spark. I did start travelling alone way back in 2001 but those trips were to Mumbai – barely 160 kilometers from home. And those trips were for educational reasons to attend and write some test series which were supposed to prep me for me pre-meds. The first solo trip I undertook – for pleasure – was a Himalayan trek to Hampta Pass in 2004. It opened a door I didn't even know existed, leading me down a path where each step unraveled another layer of understanding. I met souls who carried entire universes within them, stories woven into their eyes and laughter. One story led to another, and eventually, all of it led me here—to this very moment.

Why not create an opportunity for others to embark on their own journeys? Why not make it possible for someone, somewhere, to experience that same serendipitous magic?

And so, dear reader, if you've picked up a legitimate copy of this book—thank you. If you haven't, well, I understand. I've walked that road myself, scouring the internet for pirated texts during my college days, hungry for knowledge, too broke to afford it. I won't judge you.

But if this idea stirs something in you, if it makes your heart beat a little faster at the thought of venturing into the unknown—then maybe consider supporting it. Maybe even gift this book to someone you care about, someone you'd want to share this idea with. No pressure. Just putting it out into the universe.

01:47 AM

[IST - Indian Standard Time]

CHAPTER

15

[The images. That's the chapter.]

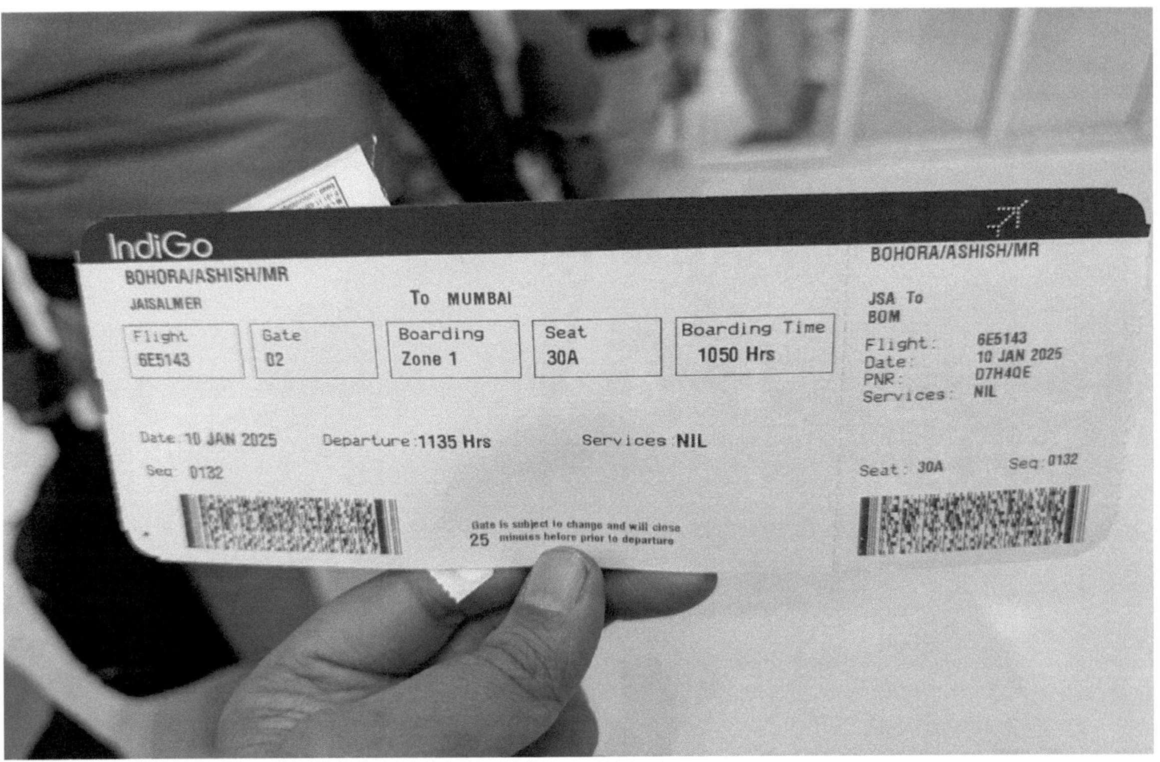

How time flies
18 years of IndiGo
#IndiabyIndiGo
रक्षा जैकेट आप की
LIFE VEST UNDER
रखिए
E SEATED

CHAPTER

CHAPTER 16

Damn.

Now that the solo travel idea has taken root in my mind, it refuses to let go. It's one thing to dream of something grand, another to actually make it happen. The more I think about it, the more I feel the pull—not just to set it up for others, but to disappear into it myself.

But here's the thing—I don't want to *work*. Not right now. Not in that way.

This phase of my life is about travel, about writing, about letting ideas flow without the weight of execution dragging them down. Managing logistics, handling sponsorships, overseeing operations—it would all become a distraction.

I know myself well enough to see that. The purity of the idea would get lost in the mechanics.

Maybe I'll find a way. Maybe I won't. *Let's see what I end up doing.*

The first day my mother and I arrived in Jaisalmer, we wandered into the fort. She, as expected, made her way into the Jain temple inside to pray. I, as expected, stayed outside, waiting.

Time stretched. Minutes felt longer than they should have. My patience thinned. I don't do temples. I don't do gods. That's never been my thing. But eventually, my restlessness won, and I stepped inside—not to pray, but to find her.

I didn't realize she had already exited through another door.

And so, for a moment, I was alone.

Something about the place—the centuries-old silence, the weight of devotion soaked into the walls—made me pause. Almost unconsciously, I joined my hands together, closed my eyes, and offered a silent prayer. To what? I don't know. To nothing, maybe. Or to everything.

Then I walked out.

Unbeknownst to me, my mother was watching from behind. She never said anything. Just smiled.

And from that day onward, ideas began to arrive. One after another.

Not just fleeting thoughts, but solid, compelling ideas. As if something had shifted. As if some unseen force had decided, *Alright then, here you go.*

As a man of science, I should chalk it up to coincidence. A trick of the mind. A psychological glitch. But still, I can't shake the feeling that somehow, *God—* or whatever that word truly represents—snuck into my story when I wasn't looking.

Funny how that happens.

Flight's taking off. Mumbai next.

Conversation to be continued later.

CHAPTER

17

Home.

That's Nashik, India. Or Nasik, if you prefer the old way of spelling it.

Funny how unplanned things happen. Like writing this chapter from home. Like the way certain numbers carve themselves into the fabric of our lives. *Seventeen.*

I was seventeen when I lost my father. It's a number that has stayed with me, woven itself into my story in ways I never could have predicted. And now, here we are—Chapter 17, written from the place where I first felt the weight of that number.

Today is a day of slow rhythms—chores, quiet moments, small indulgences.

For the first time ever, I had a special cannabis cookie at home. One of those rare treats. The kind that doesn't just alter your state of mind but shifts the entire texture of the day.

It was around 10 AM when I ate it. Read some news. Took care of a few things around the house. Then, when a gentle drowsiness crept in, I let it take me. What was meant to be a short nap turned into a deep, immersive sleep.

When I woke up, I felt fresh. Weightless. The kind of lightness that lingers even after the dreams have faded. I don't remember the specifics of what I dreamed, but I remember the feeling—peaceful, content, as if some part of my mind had wandered through a place it had been searching for.

Before I started writing this book—this journal, this conversation—I hesitated.

I wondered if I should keep contemporary events out of it, make it timeless, untethered to any specific moment in history. But then another thought surfaced: *Why not?*

Context matters. It gives meaning to everything.

Maybe, someday, someone will read this and look up the references, the time period, the things happening in the world as I write. Maybe they'll see how the backdrop of reality shaped my thoughts. Maybe they'll even try to understand *me* through these words, through these fragments of time.

After all, documenting my experiences with entheogens isn't just about personal reflection—it's about understanding what happens to the mind under their influence. And context? Context is everything when it comes to determining effects.

I am not a daily cannabis user. In fact, this year, I've only used it during my Ladakh and Jaisalmer visits. Which makes each experience more distinct, more precious.

Alcohol? That's mostly a social thing—something to sip on when catching up with friends over good food.

But if we're talking entheogens, here's my personal breakdown:

- **Cannabis** – Perfect for deep conversations, introspection, and creative flow. A social and spiritual companion.
- **Magic Mushrooms** – The ultimate for self-exploration. They don't just show you things; they *unravel* you, peeling back layers to reveal truths buried deep within. I've had them only three times, but each experience was profound.
- **Tea & Coffee** – Subtle but effective stimulants. They sharpen the mind, enhance focus. Many don't consider them entheogens, but I do—because anything that alters your state of mind *is* an entheogen, even if it's part of daily life.

- **Tobacco** – Sharpens alertness, but at a heavy cost. Highly addictive, damaging, and ultimately not worth it. Not my thing.

- **Alcohol** – A social lubricant, good for loosening up. But hangovers? A price I don't like paying. And losing control of my mind isn't something I particularly enjoy either.

- **LSD** – A mixed bag. Some trips were euphoric, deeply insightful. Others? Not so much. One bad trip amplified unresolved issues, turning them into something darker. I doubt I'll ever touch it again.

- **MDMA (Molly)** – Fantastic for bonding, for feeling connected. But the downer that follows? Intense headaches, mental fog. Not worth the price.

- **Opium** – Tried it twice. Felt relaxed, alert, but nothing extraordinary. Bitter taste. No intellectual or introspective depth. Definitely not my thing.

I tend to try an entheogen at least twice. The first time is exploration. The second is to verify, to analyze how it truly affects my mind. After that, I decide whether it's worth revisiting.

On my list for the future? **DMT, mescaline, ayahuasca.**

Will those experiences ever happen? Who knows. I don't actively seek them out—I prefer to let the universe bring them to me when the time is right. Maybe someday I'll get the chance. If I do, I hope I'll still be in the mood to document and share the experience with you.

You might think this is a one-sided conversation. But is it?

Don't you hear my voice in your head as you read? Don't you answer questions internally, forming your own thoughts and opinions in response? Don't you ever feel like you want to say something back?

Isn't that what a conversation is? Even if it happens in silence?

I hope, someday, we cross paths. That we can exchange stories and insights—not just through these pages, but in person. I'd love to know what went through your mind while reading this book.

Right now, as I write this, my room is wrapped in darkness. I'm snug under a shawl, the cold air pressing gently against the windows. The *Jaisalmer* playlist plays softly in the background—songs that captured the mood of that trip, each track a time capsule of memories.

Whenever I travel, I make it a habit to *Shazam* and save the music I hear around me. Later, when I play those songs, I'm transported back to the exact moments they were woven into.

I wish you could hear this playlist right now. Maybe, if you did, you'd feel exactly what I'm feeling. Maybe the music would stir something in you the way it does in me.

Or maybe not.

I write when I *can*, not just when I *want* to. Sometimes, those two things overlap beautifully. Other times, they exist separately—parallel lines that never meet.

And then there are moments when I don't even realize I *want* to write until I start. Words pull me in, compelling me to pour thoughts onto the page, even before I fully understand where they're going.

Maybe that's why some of these conversations feel cohesive, while others seem like scattered outliers.

Can you tell which is which?

I don't want to. Not yet.

Playing now in the background: **"I Feel Love" by Donna Summer.**

CHAPTER

18

There's a certain assumption one might make about me—that I'm always under the influence of an entheogen, lost in altered states, drifting through dimensions of thought. But that isn't true. I enjoy clarity just as much. It's just that clarity often gets consumed by life's obligations—chores, responsibilities, the mundane gears of existence that keep turning whether I like it or not. When my mind is clear, it is focused on ticking off to-do lists, handling what needs to be handled. And in those moments, I don't write.

Writing needs space. It needs a mind that isn't weighed down by errands and deadlines. It demands free flight—an untethered stream of thoughts flowing uninterrupted. That's why "Writer's Block" is real. Not because thoughts don't exist, but because they are shackled by the weight of everything else.

There have been countless times when I've had a thought so sharp, so profound, that I knew I had to tell you. I framed the words in my mind, built them up, imagined the conversation we'd have. But then life pulled me in another direction. A call, a task, a distraction. And by the time I returned to that thought, it had faded—like mist dissolving under the morning sun. Some return, triggered by a different moment entirely. Others are gone forever, lost to the ether.

[Playing now - "Blinding Lights" by The Weeknd]

I sometimes wonder—how do I make sure you hear everything I want to say? I haven't figured that out yet. Maybe I will. Maybe I won't.

Some people jot down notes, keep voice memos, scribble reminders. But that's not me. Writing in fragments disrupts the flow of thinking. To think freely, you have to let the mind wander without stopping to capture every fleeting thought.

Note-taking is good for structured writing—for shaping a story, explaining a philosophy. But for understanding the mind under the influence of entheogens, you need something else entirely. You need to let go.

Right now, I feel like telling you about the beautiful souls I've met—friends, family, the strangers who turned into stories during my travels. But those stories deserve their own space. Another day, another chapter.

[Now playing - "Just The Way You Are" by Bruno Mars]

(Interesting how this started playing right after "Skyfall" by Adele. Unexpected, but oddly fitting.)

Traveling solo has been one of the greatest gifts life has given me. The people I met, the places I wandered into, the moments that felt almost divinely orchestrated. I want others to experience that too—the way solo travel opens doors to unexpected connections, the way it teaches you about yourself in ways no book or lecture ever could. That's why I take my mother on these journeys now, to show her the world the way I see it.

[Now playing - "Kailove Chedugudu" by Naveen, SP Charan, SP Balasubrahmanyam]

The thought of creating a space for solo travelers, true explorers, has been lingering in my mind for a while. It's more than just an idea—it feels like something I was meant to do. Something I *want* to do.

But wanting something and committing to it are two different things. Making this my "life's work" would mean diving headfirst into logistics, planning, structure. And structure, as you know, has never been my strong suit. It requires time, dedication, and—most terrifyingly—routine.

Will I do it? I don't know. My heart refuses to let go of the idea, but my mind keeps reminding me of the weight it carries.

[Now playing - "Sang Rahiyo" by Jasleen Royal and Ujjwal Kashyap]

Time will tell. It always does.

I don't dislike working—I actually enjoy it when it's on my own terms. But I have no desire to be tied down. I haven't taken up a job in years, not because I can't, but because I *choose* not to. There's always someone else who needs that opportunity more. There's always another reason—freedom, mobility, the avoidance of the mundane. And I've learned that just because you *can* start something doesn't mean you should. Starting something just for the sake of it, only to be bound by it, isn't how I want to live.

But then again, if the universe brings the right people, the right circumstances, who knows? I might just do it.

[Now playing - "Papi (Bhabi)" by Eden Shalev]

I live by one simple rule—if it's meant to be, it will be.

[Now playing - "Love Theme" from The Godfather]

A fitting end to this chapter. A quiet, contemplative close.

This entire playlist—the "Jaisalmer" playlist—has been playing in the background as I write. I wonder if you'll listen to it too. Maybe, for a brief moment, we'll share the same headspace. Maybe you'll hear these songs and feel something similar to what I feel right now.

If you do, my personal recommendation:

["Phoenix" by Yatao.]

Listen to it. You'll understand why.

CHAPTER

CHAPTER 19

The cookie from Jaisalmer—another whole one this time. I ate it about two hours ago, sometime before I began writing the last chapter.

Nothing yet. No waves, no shifts. Just a quiet wait.

It's 22:52 as I write this, the night stretching ahead, still undecided on whether it wants to be ordinary or extraordinary.

Distractions trickle in. WhatsApp messages flashing on the screen, little digital voices pulling me in different directions. Conversations that don't demand urgency but linger like static in the background.

(For those unfamiliar with 'WhatsApp'—a quick online search should suffice. Assuming, of course, that in the time and space you exist, the internet remains free, unfiltered, and truth is still accessible. If not, well... I hope you find another way to know the things you wish to know.)

I turn my attention back to the page, staring at the blankness, waiting for the words to arrive. But my mind is quiet, unusually so. No grand revelations, no intricate thoughts weaving themselves into sentences. Just… silence. A blank wall where something should be.

23:03. January 11, 2025.

I glance at the remaining cookies, considering.

Should I try another?

CHAPTER

The plan had been simple. A train ride, a seamless transition from one place to another, an easy passage to Jaisalmer, where the golden sands would greet us as we bid farewell to one year and embraced the next. But as life often does, it decided to throw in a detour—a missed connecting train.

For a brief moment, standing on that platform, uncertainty loomed. The weight of disrupted plans, the unpredictability of what lay ahead. But before frustration could settle, something else took its place—kindness. The kind that restores faith in the very fabric of human connection.

Strangers—locals, their faces weathered with wisdom and generosity—stepped forward, offering directions, advice, and the simple reassurance that we were not stranded, only rerouted. They pointed us toward a different path, one that wound through the roads rather than the rails.

And so, our journey reshaped itself. From Ahmedabad, we boarded a bus, only to switch to another, and then yet another. Three buses, each filled with unfamiliar faces, conversations in passing, the scent of roadside chai mingling with the dry desert air. With every mile, exhaustion should have crept in, but instead, there was an odd sense of adventure, of surrendering to the unexpected.

Finally, Jaisalmer. A city carved from golden sandstone, waiting for us under the vast, open sky. The journey had not gone as planned, but perhaps it had gone exactly as it was meant to. We had arrived—not just by buses and roads, but by the goodwill of those who reminded us that even in moments of uncertainty, kindness is a compass that never fails.

And so, with weary feet but light hearts, we stepped into the last days of 2024, ready to welcome 2025—not just with celebration, but with gratitude.

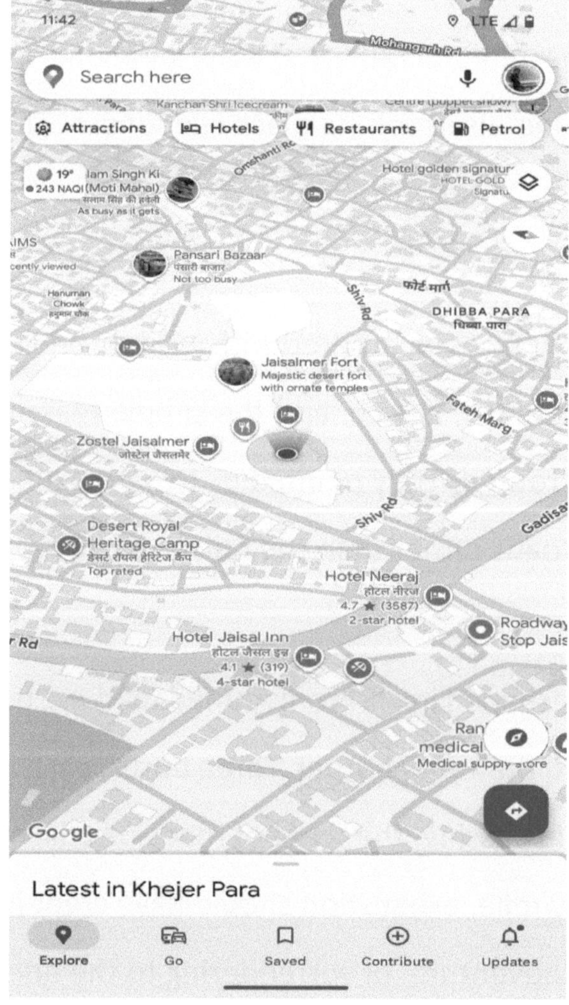

I picked up the pen—or rather, opened my notes—on January 6th. Not because nothing had happened before that, but because that's the day I finally wrestled with laziness and won.

But between December 25th and January 6th? Oh, plenty happened.

The cannabis-fueled conversations began right from day one. Old friends, new faces, friends of friends—what I like to call the *Joint Family*. A loosely connected tribe, bound not by blood, but by a shared love for good company, deep musings, and the gentle haze of a well-rolled joint passed from hand to hand under desert skies.

Then came day three.

The *bhang* from Doctor Cafe was different. Not just another high, not just another trip—it felt like it unlatched a hidden door in my mind, pried open some blocked-off corridor that had been gathering dust for who knows how long. I could almost hear the hinges creak as thoughts, old and new, began flowing freely, unrestrained. A gentle but powerful unlocking.

As for the New Year's Eve party? Fairly standard. The usual mix of food, drinks, music—laughter swelling and fading in waves as people danced their way into 2025. But I made a conscious choice that night. No cannabis. No blending of entheogens. The mind, after all, deserves to savor each experience in its own right, without muddling the edges.

So I welcomed the new year in clarity, with a steady mind and a light heart—knowing that soon enough, I would drift once again into the depths of introspection, into the places only entheogens seem to reach.

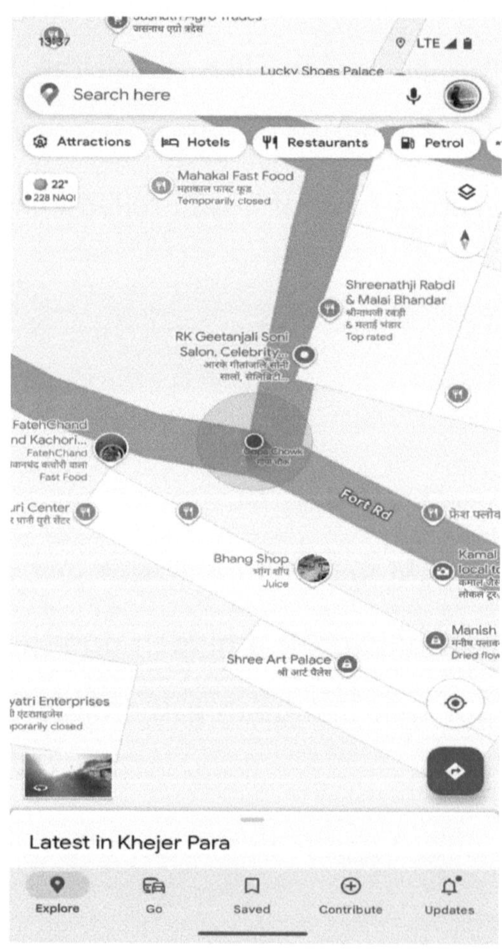

I started slow.

With both *bhang* and the special cookie, I took measured steps—just a small amount at first, watching, listening, feeling. Observing their effects as they rippled through both body and mind, like dipping a toe into unknown waters before wading deeper. With time, I adjusted—upping the dose or strength gradually, testing my boundaries, searching for that elusive *sweet spot* where clarity, insight, and euphoria aligned without tipping into excess.

I've learned to be patient with entheogens.

There was only one time I dived in headfirst without first mapping the terrain—2012, my first encounter with magic mushrooms. I had no clue how much would be the right amount for me. So I trusted a friend's recommendation, surrendered to the unknown. The impact was phenomenal—unlike anything I had ever experienced. But looking back, I know it was a risk.

See, I don't like jumping into deep water without first finding my feet. I believe in exploring limits, yes—but with knowledge, awareness, and preferably the presence of experienced guides who can anchor you in case the trip turns tricky.

That's where smokable cannabis holds an advantage. You find your threshold quickly, adjusting in real time, able to stop precisely when you need to. Ingestibles, though, demand patience. They must pass through the digestive system, seep into the bloodstream, and only then do their magic. By the time you realize you've had too much, there's no turning back.

And then, there's tolerance.

The moment you stop hitting your *sweet spot*—even when taking the same type and amount of an entheogen—it's a warning sign. Your body and brain are building resistance. Push beyond that, and dependency lurks around the corner. When that happens, the answer is simple: stop. Take a break. Reset.

For me, that break is usually 30 to 50 weeks at minimum. A long enough stretch to clear my system, reset my mind, and let my sensitivity return naturally.

Remember the last chapter? That moment of indecision—wondering whether or not to have another cookie? I had it. The sweet spot came, but later than usual. Slightly delayed, slightly dulled—a whisper that it's time for another break.

So, I'll step back from cannabis for a while. Let the mind breathe, let the body rest.

But before I go—if you ever get the chance, try cannabis in the desert.

The golden light of the setting sun stretching across the dunes. The hard, cool sand beneath your feet. The quiet—so deep it hums in your ears. Camels grazing nearby, silhouettes against the horizon. A perfect, infinite stillness.

I did it this time. And I loved every moment of it.

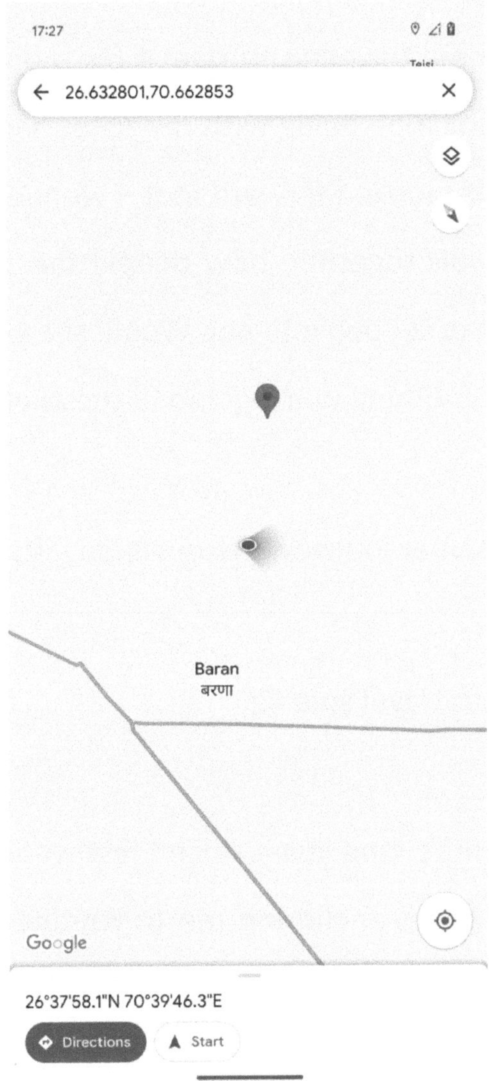

I wanted to stay longer in Jaisalmer.

Something about that place—its golden sands, the slow-burning sunsets, the way time stretches and bends in the desert air—made me wish for a few more days, maybe weeks. But plans had already been set in motion, and life, as always, had its way of pulling me back.

Mum had her Schengen visa appointment in Mumbai.

This would be her first time traveling abroad. A big moment, though not a solo adventure—this time, she'd be going with my sister and Maggie. A tour, more than true travel, but still, I looked forward to it. I wondered how much she had absorbed from our travels together, how deeply the stories, the places, the essence of movement had seeped into her. Would she see the world differently now? Would she find something unexpected in the experience?

And while she sets off on her journey, the universe gifts me a window.

A long-awaited chance to travel solo again.

It's been three years. Three long years since I last wandered alone, without a plan, without familiar voices anchoring me to routine. Familial obligations—important, necessary, deeply loved—had made it difficult to break away often. But when the stars align, when the chance presents itself, I don't just take it.

I *go.*

And not just go—I *fly.*

If you know what I mean.

14:34
5G
Search here
Work
Hotels
Restaurants
Petrol
Att
Petals of Joy
um Flower Shop
29°
159 NAQI
Phoenix Palladium
Biggest Luxury
Watch Brands
Lower Parel Station
लोअर परळ स्टे
Manyavar & Mohey
Wedding Ready
with Manyavar
Lower Parel
entre
Overhead
Water Tank
Masque
मास्क
VFS Global Georgia
Visa Application Center
Recently viewed
Google
Dhobi Ghat
धोबी घाट, मुंबई
500 ft
200 m
Latest in Mahalakshmi
Hotels nearby
Explore
Go
Saved
Contribute
Updates

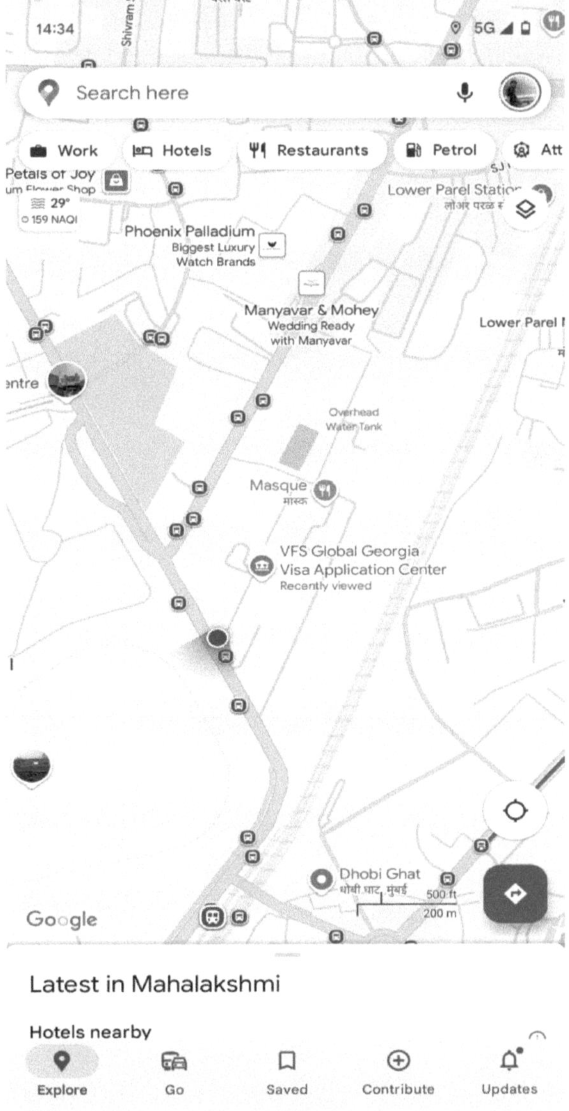

Ch. 20

[The End]

CHAPTER

(22-1) = 21

I always carried a weight—a gnawing sense of guilt that never truly left me.

My father, my uncles—generations of men before them—were all unwaveringly hardworking. They built their lives with the sweat of their brows and the relentless force of their will. My sister and cousins followed suit, each carving their own path with discipline and determination.

And then there was me.

From an early age, I knew I was different. Hard work, in the traditional sense, never appealed to me. What fascinated me was the realm of thought—ideas that could unravel the mysteries of existence, insights that could illuminate the depths of human nature. I thrived in learning, in questioning, in exploring, but never in grinding away at tasks I had no passion for.

For the longest time, I believed I would follow in my father's footsteps and become a doctor. Some part of me still clings to that vision—who knows, maybe one day I'll study medicine. But as time went on, I realized that my guilt stemmed from something deeper: the feeling that I wasn't contributing to society in a tangible way.

I hated the idea of working a conventional job under someone else. My attempts at entrepreneurship—startups born out of passion—had all met their end, not for lack of success, but because I had no interest in the endless burden of management, structure, and 'professional execution.' The moment the work became about logistics instead of creation, my heart left it.

Instead, I was drawn to what people like to call 'smart work'—the kind that doesn't shackle you to an office or a routine, the kind that only requires a sharp mind and a well-honed intuition. Teaching came close. I loved it. But I never wanted it to define my career.

Law intrigued me the most. I saw it as a powerful tool—an understanding of the very fabric that governs society. So, I pursued it, cracked the entrance exam for one of India's top law schools in Delhi, and immersed myself in the study of justice and governance.

But I never wanted to be a lawyer. For me, law was an intellectual pursuit, not a profession. I wanted to decode its intricacies, to wield it when necessary, but never to be bound by it. The reality of the Indian judicial system—its inefficiencies, its archaic absurdities—left me deeply disillusioned. That, along with my growing frustration with the uninspired, mechanical nature of university examinations, sealed my decision to walk away. I quit in my final semester.

By then, the thought had already settled in my mind: I was a failure.

I saw myself as a man merely coasting through life on the fortune of inheritance, incapable of offering anything meaningful to the grand human story. So, I made peace with it. I decided I would simply live wisely—manage whatever blessings I had, travel the world, and let life unfold as it pleased.

But the universe had other plans.

A cousin, noticing my obsession with documenting my thoughts and experiences, suggested I start writing. "Leave behind something for others to read," he said. I dismissed the idea. That was about two or three years ago—I can't recall exactly when.

Then, in Leh, I met a stranger who would soon become a friend. Our first encounter was purely accidental—one of those serendipitous moments the universe orchestrates. Over shared conversations, crisp mountain air, and a bit of cannabis, she saw something in me that I hadn't. "You tell stories well," she pointed out. "You should write."

I brushed it off, attributing it to the haze of intoxication rather than any real ability of mine.

And then, a few months later, the universe nudged me again. This time, it happened in Jaisalmer. Another friend—also a traveler, but more importantly, a writer—told me, in no uncertain terms, to stop being lazy and just start. "Write about whatever you want," she urged.

It was the third sign. And this time, I listened.

Here we are. I did end up writing, and you did end up reading.

For the first time, I knew exactly what I wanted to put into words. I wanted to document the beauty, the revelations, the profound truths that entheogens have gifted me. I wanted to show those who come after us how these substances—when used wisely—can open doors to experiences beyond imagination. But more than that, I wanted to leave behind a piece of myself, something that might matter to someone, someday.

Just like that, I found a purpose—something I could do for the rest of my life without a second thought.

And just like that, the guilt began to fade.

The universe has a strange way of orchestrating connections. You could be walking alone in a foreign city, sipping chai at a nameless roadside stall, when suddenly, a stranger sits beside you. A conversation starts—effortlessly, as if it was always meant to happen. Maybe it's the air of solo travel, the weightlessness of being untethered, that allows souls to recognize each other beyond the masks of everyday life.

I've always been fascinated by this—how certain people, certain conversations, arrive at the exact moment they are supposed to. It's as if there's an invisible thread linking wanderers, seekers, thinkers—those who travel not just across landscapes but within themselves. This idea of *connecting souls on solo trips* lingers in my mind, hovering at the edges of possibility. Could it be another purpose waiting to unfold?

I don't know. Maybe it'll remain an idea, a passing thought that never solidifies into action, just like so many other ideas before it. Or maybe—just maybe—it'll turn into something real, the way writing unexpectedly did. Time will tell. Only time can tell.

But for now, I know one thing for certain.

I think I might have figured out where I want to end this book.

It's strange, this realization—like reaching the final pages of a chapter, knowing that the next one is waiting to be written. There's an urgency to it, a sense of alignment. If I stop here, if I let this book go out into the world now, it means I can step fully into the next phase of my journey. It means I can live more, experience more, and most importantly, record the next chapters of my (entheogenic?) life as they unfold in real time.

Because the story isn't over.

Not yet.

LiVE MOMENTS before
you start
CAPTURING them

CHAPTER

CHAPTER 22

There are so many stories I wish I could share with you. Especially the entheogenic ones—the kind that bend time, deepen connections, and reveal layers of existence we often overlook. But like I mentioned earlier, stories without context and characters don't carry the same weight. And out of respect for those who were a part of them, I won't tell them. Not just yet.

I want to tell you about the mishaps I had in 2018 and 2022—the ones that changed the way I saw myself, the world, and my relationship with cannabis. If the doctors were right, they were *cannabis mishaps*. But what if they weren't? What if those experiences were something else entirely? What if they were just an unraveling of my mind in ways I wasn't prepared for?

I want to tell you exactly what was going through my head, the thoughts that led me down certain paths, the emotions that surged through me as I made decisions—some reckless, some deeply intentional. But more than that, I want you to hear it from those who were affected by my actions.

I want you to read or hear their version of events first. Because only then will you have an unbiased perspective. Only then will you see the full picture, unswayed by my words or justifications.

Maybe you'll never get to know what happened. Maybe this book won't reach enough people for those stories to surface. Maybe they'll remain buried, fading into the past, becoming nothing more than whispers lost in time. And if that's the case, who cares? Some stories are meant to disappear. But if they do resurface, I hope they give you the clarity to discern what *not* to do when exploring certain substances, certain situations, and certain states of mind.

Who knows—maybe someday, if the universe wills, I will tell you those stories myself.

But for now, let me tell you about something I *can* share.

The best cannabis I have ever smoked in my life came from Uttarakhand, from a little roadside shop opposite the gates of the *Jim Corbett National Park Office* in Ramnagar. It was 2011. I was backpacking with a friend, soaking in the freedom of the road, when we stumbled upon it.

That stuff was pure magic. I bought about 20 grams of it—or was it 200? Memory's a little hazy. All I know is I paid a mere ₹300 for it. Getting it through airport security on my way back to Pune was a whole other adventure (a story for another time).

I rolled joints with that stuff—no tobacco, just pure, unadulterated cannabis. Two or three puffs were enough to send me into a state of absolute bliss. I'd stub out the remaining joint and save it for the next Sunday. Back then, I was teaching kids at a government school, so I kept my cannabis use limited—once a week, every Sunday. A ritual. A reward. A moment of solitude.

That 2011 Uttarakhand cannabis lasted me nearly nine months, even after sharing it with friends. I haven't come across anything like it since. Everything else—local weed from Jaisalmer, imported strains from California, even some high-quality Thai cannabis—has felt *off* in some way. Either too stoning, too chemical-laden, or lacking the sheer euphoria of the stuff I found in the hills of Uttarakhand.

But the real story from that trip? It happened deep inside Jim Corbett National Park.

It was late at night. We had arrived that evening and were staying at the National Park Guest House. I needed to confirm the timing for our safari the next morning, so I wandered over to the drivers' cabin. As I approached, laughter—loud, uninhibited, *infectious*—echoed from inside.

I knocked.

The door creaked open, and I was immediately hit by a thick, swirling cloud of ganja smoke. The room was bathed in a dim orange glow from a single bulb hanging from the ceiling. Beds lined the walls—four or five of them, I think—but the real scene was in the center of the room.

A group of safari drivers sat cross-legged on the floor, passing around joints and bongs, telling stories that had them howling with laughter. It was the kind of laughter that makes you laugh too, even when you don't know the joke. The kind of warmth that pulls you in, makes you feel like you've stumbled into the *right* place, at the *right* time.

I knew instantly—I was in good company.

One of them gestured for me to come in, handing me a freshly rolled joint. The invitation was unspoken but understood. I accepted.

The entire night unraveled in that smoky cabin. Stories flowed like the river outside. They spoke of tigers and spirits, of near-misses and strange encounters deep in the forest. Some tales were hilarious, others haunting. But every single one of them was told with an energy that made you *believe*.

I don't remember everything we talked about, but I remember how it felt— like a moment outside of time. Like I had stepped into a hidden pocket of the universe, a place reserved only for those who find it by accident.

I left the cabin just as the first hints of dawn began to stretch across the sky, carrying with me the echoes of laughter and the scent of burnt cannabis on my clothes.

There are more stories like this. So many more. Some I might tell you if we ever cross paths.

Like the night of October 2, 2015, when I found myself sharing cannabis with a Delhi Police officer near Lodhi Gardens at 2 AM.

Remind me to tell you that one someday.

I wonder if I'll ever get to meet the souls who read this book—not as fans, but as fellow travelers, thinkers, and seekers. I wonder if I'll sit across from someone who, years from now, picks up this book, connects with these words, and feels compelled to find me. Not to ask for an autograph or a selfie, but to swap stories over some good cannabis, to share laughter in a dimly lit room where time slows down and the world outside ceases to exist.

If that ever happens, I'll know the universe was listening.

And if not?

Well, the universe has a way of bringing things full circle, in its own time, in its own way.

CHAPTER

23 - THE CHOICE BETWEEN NATURE AND SYNTHETICS

21:03

Let me tell you why I prefer organics.

It's not just about the high—it never has been. It's about something deeper, something older than civilization itself. We evolved alongside nature. The plants, the fungi, the elements—they have been here long before us, shaping ecosystems, interacting with life forms, and, in some cases, whispering their secrets to the human mind.

Natural substances—entheogens like cannabis, psilocybin mushrooms, and even certain cacti—contain a symphony of compounds, working together in ways we still don't fully understand. They are complex, balanced, and in harmony with the biological systems we've inherited over millennia. Our bodies recognize them. They metabolize them. They know how to handle them, as if on some ancestral level, a familiarity lingers between us and these plants.

But synthetics? That's a different story.

Synthetics are precision weapons, not natural symphonies. Designed to target specific molecules, they isolate, amplify, and override, often ignoring the intricate interplay of compounds that nature so effortlessly weaves together. They don't *work with* the body; they *override* it. And that's what makes them dangerous.

They can be highly addictive. They can hijack the mind. They can lead you down a path where curiosity turns into compulsion, where exploration turns into enslavement.

I never want to go down that path.

I've never touched heroin, never snorted cocaine, never even considered fentanyl. Not because I fear them in the way society teaches us to fear substances, but because I *understand* them. I understand their power, their grip, their ability to rewire a person from the inside out.

Even amphetamines—I've never tried them. And I doubt I ever will.

For me, it has never been about *playing* with my mind. It's about *understanding* it. It's about peeling back layers of perception, about exploring how certain entheogens interact with my consciousness. But only the natural ones. Only those that have stood the test of time, that have been used by seekers, shamans, and mystics long before modern chemistry turned to isolation and synthesis.

Of course, if I come across something familiar—like cannabis or mushrooms—I indulge again. But always responsibly. Always with the awareness that these substances are tools, not crutches.

LSD and molly are the only synthetics I have ever tried.

And I'm still not sure if Adderall counts.

I took it once during law school, on the recommendation of a friend. Sleep-deprived and desperate for focus before an exam, I gave in to curiosity. Popped a pill. Waited.

Nothing.

At least, nothing remarkable. My mind didn't sharpen into a blade, my focus didn't become laser-like, my energy didn't surge. If anything, it was forgettable. Whatever effect it had was so subtle that I never bothered with it again.

LSD, though?

That's a different story.

LSD is something I genuinely believe everyone should try at least once in their life. Not for the high, not for the visuals, but for the sheer *perspective shift* it brings. It stretches reality, bends time, and dissolves the walls we spend our whole lives building. It doesn't just alter the mind—it *reveals* it.

Molly, on the other hand… I could take it or leave it.

The comedown was enough to put me off. That hollow, drained feeling that follows the euphoria—it wasn't worth it. Twice was enough. I never touched it again.

There's a lesson in that, I suppose.

Some substances open doors. Others close them.

And some, if you're not careful, don't just close doors—they lock them behind you.

CHAPTER

THE WALRUS, THE ELEPHANT, AND THE WEIGHT OF FREEDOM

22:49

I took a break from this book. Not sure exactly when. Time slips away so easily when the mind drifts between reflection and routine. Some of that time went into thinking. Some into daily chores. And just like that, the pause stretched longer than I had intended.

But now, here I am again.

A few minutes ago, I finished my first book. A one-pager. Strange, isn't it? A book in a single page. But depth isn't measured in length—just as beauty is in the eye of the beholder, depth lies in the diver's ability.

That book had come to me first, even before this one. A whisper before the storm.

It is titled—**"Untitled."**

For a while, I toyed with the idea of giving this book the same name. It carried a certain poetic irony, an open-ended truth that I found compelling. But after some thought, I realized *Untitled* belonged to the other one. This one had a different story to tell.

This one is **"Confessions of a CannDid Mind."**

(Fitting, don't you think? I do. I *Cann(abis)*, I *Did*, and that made me **CannDid**.)

There's a story I could tell you about that—one tied to a memory I hold dear. But that tale? That one, I will share only when we meet in person. And only if you're curious enough to remind me.

The cover of this book is special, too.

There's a story behind the image. A reason for the stamp I chose. But some stories are best left waiting for the right questions. If curiosity ever strikes you, ask me. Until then, it remains a secret.

As the years have passed, I've noticed a shift in myself.

My **isolophilia** has been on the rise.

Not that I don't enjoy good company—I do. But my love for my own company has grown stronger. Once upon a time, I thrived in social circles, reveling in the dance of conversation and the energy of crowds. I was an extrovert then. Now? Now, I find more joy in absorbing, listening, reflecting.

A friend once asked me: *If you weren't human, what animal would you be?*

Not *which animal I wanted to be*, but which one I *was.*

Without much thought, I answered—**walrus.**

At the time, it felt right. My increasing laziness, my expanding girth, my quiet fondness for tusks—it all pointed in that direction. But today, I learned something new. Walruses, it turns out, are deeply social creatures. Gregarious. Playful.

It made me smile.

The Universe has a way of guiding us, doesn't it? First, it makes you say something without knowing why. Then it nudges you to ponder over it. And finally, it leads you to a realization—one that was waiting for you all along.

I used to socialize effortlessly. Now, my **introvert-to-extrovert ratio** has shifted, and I couldn't be happier about it.

(But if I could *choose* an animal to become? An elephant, without question. For many reasons. Wisdom among them.)

I have always been an autodidact when it comes to emotions.

I once believed I understood them. That I had a firm grasp on what love was, what heartbreak felt like, what hope and despair truly meant. But I was wrong.

The women who passed through my life—whether they meant to or not—became my teachers. They showed me the depths of sentiment, the weight of turmoil, the quiet resilience of hope. They revealed love to me in its rawest forms. And in doing so, they also taught me something else.

They taught me that I *did not want* emotional entanglements.

By the time I graduated from what I now call the **Emotion Academy**, I knew. I wanted no bonds. No anchors. No responsibilities of the sentimental kind.

Will that ever change? I don't know.

But at this moment, in this life I've carved out for myself, I see no reason to let go of my solitude. This **unmarried bachelorhood**, this **freedom**, this **isolophilia**—it brings me peace. It keeps me light.

Because in the end, life is all about *letting go*.

I love kids.

As long as they aren't mine.

I've known this about myself since I was a teenager. I never wanted the weight of parenthood on my shoulders. Never wanted to be responsible for raising another life. And now, looking back at the choices I've made, I can see why.

You've had a glimpse into my mind by now. You understand the way my thoughts roam, the way I choose solitude over attachment. Why would I drag a beautiful soul into this turbulence? Why would I take on a role that demands sacrifices I am unwilling to make?

I don't think I'd ever make a good partner.

A good friend? Perhaps. A good confidant? Maybe. But a good partner? That requires a kind of selflessness I do not possess.

And yet—

One can never predict the whims of life, can they?

There have been moments when I've sworn **never**—only for fate to laugh and make me do exactly what I thought I wouldn't.

The lesson? Life is uncertain.

The only thing we can do is live it while we can.

And when we can't—we must learn to let go.

(A particularly difficult lesson for me, once upon a time.)

Remember when I told you I figured out when I'd finish this book?

Well, I think I know now.

This volume will end when I run out of those special cookies I brought back from Jaisalmer. When the last crumb is gone, I will wrap this up. Until the next entheogenic journey calls.

(And no, tea, coffee, and tobacco don't count. Those are mundane entheogens, too weak to stir the depths of wisdom. I'll write again when something truly worthy emerges.)

[PS: This is not the end. Not yet. The cookies will last a while longer. So keep reading.]

[End of Session (or Chapter) 24]

01:01 AM – **Monday, Jan 13**

(Time to go back to reading. And, of course, wasting time on the internet.)

CHAPTER

SESSION 25

I don't know when you—whoever you are—reading this book, were (or will be) born. But I wonder what kind of world you inhabit.

The times we live in feel unprecedented, veering into strange and uneasy territories. The world tilts rightward, nations shrink into isolation, and the warmth once reserved for strangers seems to be fading. Borders harden, not just on maps but in minds.

While in Jaisalmer, I met travelers from different corners of the world, and though each carried a different accent, a different passport, the same unspoken tension lingered in all their conversations. Wars raged somewhere far away, yet their echoes reached even into desert fireside discussions. The air was thick with the weight of uncertainty.

This chapter isn't about my political stance. My thoughts, my leanings—you'll find those scattered in my LinkedIn comments and discussions, if the platform still exists when you chance upon this book. If my profile remains, still floating in the digital ether, you might gather some breadcrumbs of my perspective.

But I do worry. I worry for Maggie. I worry for the next generation.

I was fortunate to be born in a time of relative peace, a time when globalization was expanding, not retreating. I saw, firsthand, how good leadership could shape a nation, how a single policy could alter the destinies of millions, if not billions. Will the children of tomorrow get to witness such progress? Or will they inherit a world far more fragmented than the one I knew?

[A fleeting, absurd thought]—Back in my PhD days at the National Chemical Laboratory (NCL) in Pune, I once entertained the idea of *cannabis grenades*. Drop one in a war zone, let the soldiers on both sides light up, and watch as weapons are abandoned for laughter and music. No war, only peace. Naturally, the idea never saw the light of day. My friends burst into laughter when I pitched it. "Too far-fetched," they said.

[Ironically], some of my most patentable ideas came after a good session of pot. But I never truly wanted to pursue a PhD. I enrolled only because I wanted to extend my MTech research for another year. The stipend was an added incentive.

My ideas, however, remained locked within academic proposals, never materializing into anything tangible. A different life, a different time.

Of all the things I do, keeping up with news and current affairs has been a constant. I might detach from many things, but never from the pulse of the world. If anything, my paranoia-ridden 2016-2022 phase—where cannabis collided with ideology—was proof of how deep my interest ran.

It's not just because of my financial investments, though keeping an eye on global shifts does help safeguard them. It's more about my fascination with leadership, governance, constitutions, and the sheer unpredictability of geopolitics. That this awareness also aids in smart investment decisions is just a fortunate byproduct.

[Maybe that's why] politics and world affairs dominate this chapter. That was what I had been reading just before I picked up my pen. Thoughts spill over from the last thing the mind consumed, don't they?

What comes next—for the world, for me, for you—I do not know. No one does. If only a time machine existed, allowing us to peer into the ripples of today's choices, to see which wars ended, which governments collapsed, which leaders rose and fell. But alas, no such machine yet. Only time will tell.

For now, I must wrap this chapter. There's another task waiting—a synopsis for this book. Something literary agents will need if I am to find a home for these words in the publishing world. Not an easy feat, considering this book is a genre-defying creature, a hybrid of thoughts and experiences stitched together into a single, unpredictable tapestry.

We'll see how that goes.

Until next time—Adios, amigos.

19:14

CHAPTER

SESSION 26

This book will do one of two things—it will either deepen your skepticism and distrust toward entheogens, or it will nudge you, ever so slightly, toward the idea of trying them. Maybe just once. Just to see.

And if you're someone who already ventures into the entheogenic realms from time to time, I hope this book serves as an additional perspective—a data point in your ongoing exploration. Because that's all experience is in the end, isn't it?

More data. More patterns. More things to decode.

Every mind experiences entheogens differently. The variables are endless—your state of mind at the time, the food in your system, the dose, the strain, the setting, even the people you're with. No two trips are ever identical. Even within the same mind.

Looking back at my own history, cannabis was both a silent witness and an accomplice to my biggest screw-ups. And yet, in the same breath, it was also present during some of my most profound connections, my most unforgettable memories.

So, the question remains—did cannabis *change* me, or did it simply amplify what was already within me?

I don't have an answer to that. Not yet.

Maybe it takes a lifetime to truly understand the long-term effects of something. Maybe the answers only emerge in retrospect, in the stories we tell ourselves decades later. What I do know is this—I will keep experimenting. Responsibly, of course. For as long as I can.

Writing all of this down, documenting these experiences, is my way of gathering personal data. A long-term study of my own consciousness, if you will. Over time, as these *CannDid Confessions* accumulate, I hope they offer me insight into my own evolving mind.

And if you, dear reader, find yourself warming up to the idea of trying an entheogen after reading this, my advice is simple—take it slow. Steady. Do your homework. Research thoroughly before you even consider taking the plunge.

More specifically, start by looking into the *negatives* first. The bad trips. The horror stories. The things that can go wrong. Understand them well, because knowledge is a safety net. If you know what to expect when things go south, you stand a better chance of pulling yourself out of it. It might just save you from spiraling into panic if the trip takes a darker turn.

Now, here's where I differ from most—I don't research the *good* effects. I prefer to let those come as a surprise, unfolding naturally, without expectation. I want the positive revelations to introduce themselves, not arrive pre-scripted by someone else's experience. Maybe that's just me. You'll have to decide what works for you.

Cannabis is a good starting point. If you're a complete beginner, I'd recommend *smoking* rather than *ingesting*. When you smoke, the effects hit almost instantly. This means you can pace yourself, stopping when it feels right. Edibles, on the other hand, creep up on you—often when you least expect it—and by then, there's no turning back.

That's how I started. That's what worked for me.

Another key recommendation—*company matters.* Surround yourself with people you trust. If possible, have someone with you who has experience with the particular entheogen you're trying. They won't just guide you through it; they'll also know what to do if things go sideways. A good trip-sitter is like an anchor in uncharted waters.

With mushrooms, however, the approach is different. Unlike cannabis, where you can control the intensity by stopping at will, mushrooms demand surrender. You have to let go. To trust the flow of emotions, memories, and sensations as they rise and fall like waves. That's the only way to experience their full depth. Resistance only leads to turbulence.

And if, in the midst of it all, you happen to remember this book—if a particular thought or vision stirs something in you—look me up. I'd love to hear about your trip. Your story. Your data. It all adds to the ever-expanding puzzle.

[A passing thought]—As I write this, it occurs to me that I wouldn't want Maggie, or my other nieces and nephews, stumbling upon this book until they're at least 25. I hope they don't. And if they do, I hope they wait. Wait until they're truly independent in thought and action. Until they understand themselves enough to make such choices with clarity.

[Another passing thought]—Right now, as I put these words down for you, I'm also running a small experiment in parallel. A focus-strengthening exercise. I have music playing in the background, but I'm making sure it doesn't seep into my writing, doesn't influence my words. A simple test of discipline. Try it sometime—it's more challenging than it sounds.

No, I won't share what I'm listening to. Let your imagination fill in the blanks.

...

Fine. One song. Just one.

Now playing—*"Without You" by Oh Wonder.*

[Happy listening.]

CHAPTER

So begins the 27th.

It's a little chilly tonight in Nashik—not the kind of cold that bites, but the kind that gently nudges you to wrap yourself in a woolen shawl. Just enough to make you feel the season, yet not enough to shut the window. I keep it open, letting the winter air carry its whispers into the room. In another five to seven weeks, this chill will fade into warmth, like all things transient in life.

Do you remember what I mentioned back in Chapter 25? About the synopsis I was supposed to write for literary agencies? Well, I didn't. Instead, I turned to OpenAI's ChatGPT, curious to see how it would perceive *Confessions of a CannDid Mind*. It didn't disappoint. With about 90% accuracy, it summarized my thoughts, my journey, my musings.

Here's what it said:

"Confessions of a CannDid Mind is an introspective narrative exploring the life, thoughts, and experiences of the author, Ashish Bohora (Shashi). Presented as a free-flowing journal, it delves into themes of self-discovery, philosophy, and experimentation with entheogens (substances like cannabis and magic mushrooms) that inspire creative and reflective thinking.

Bohora reflects on his personal evolution, relationships, and societal norms while emphasizing a life unconstrained by traditional ambitions. He begins by disclaiming the fictional nature of the anecdotes, asserting they are creative constructs, although the narrative feels deeply personal. Through his experiences with travel, philosophy, and entheogens, he questions the meaning of life, the value of societal validation, and the nature of consciousness itself.

Ultimately, Confessions of a CannDid Mind is a raw, unstructured chronicle of a life lived on one's own terms, marked by deep introspection, experimentation, and a quest for understanding both the self and the universe."

Not bad, right?

But here's what it missed—the 10% that no AI, no algorithm, no external observer could ever capture.

This book, this narration, this entire stream of thought—none of it would have unfolded the way it did if it weren't for the presence of entheogens in my life. The special cannabis cookies from Jaisalmer, the mushroom-fueled contemplations, the altered perspectives that turned ordinary experiences into profound revelations. That's the missing piece.

This *CannDid Confession* isn't just a book. It's an experiment in raw, unfiltered thought. A record of how a mind flows when it is free from inhibition, when it surrenders to curiosity, when it lets go of rigid structure and embraces the chaos of true creativity.

Journaling this way is a blessing. Years from now, if I ever look back at these words, they will serve as a time capsule—one that doesn't just preserve memories but also maps the evolution of my thoughts, my beliefs, my understanding of self. If nothing else, they will remind me of who I was, and who I became.

I have loved every moment of writing this. I didn't edit. I didn't go back and refine my words, didn't correct my punctuation, didn't smooth out the rough edges. With one exception—Chapter 8. Everything else remains raw, untouched, just as it poured out of me. That's the beauty of it. That's the *truth* of it.

It makes this book feel like a conversation—one where I must rely on my own memory to recall if I've told you something before or not. A dialogue, not a monologue. A continuous thread of thought between you and me, even if we exist in different moments in time.

Over the years, I've wrestled with the idea of fate and free will. As a younger man, I believed in self-determination. I was convinced we shape our own destiny, carve our own path, control our own outcomes. But life, with all its unpredictable twists, has humbled me.

I've learned that efforts are never one-sided. That no matter how hard you push, the universe must push back in alignment for things to work out. If fate wills it, things fall into place. If it doesn't, all the effort in the world can't make something happen.

And so, I find peace in surrendering to what *is*. Not passively, but with acceptance. With trust.

Science still holds my heart, though. I am, at my core, someone who questions, who observes, who seeks evidence. I try to find proof of fate, proof of meaning, proof of patterns in the randomness. And ironically, that proof never lies in grand cosmic signs—it lies in the smallest of moments. The quiet synchronicities. The chance encounters. The choices that seem random until you step back and see the invisible threads connecting them.

Are coincidences really coincidences? Or are they echoes of something bigger, something we can't quite grasp?

There have been times in my life when I wished for something with all my heart. And it happened.

So right now, if I had one wish, it would be this—that you read this book, and that somewhere, somehow, our paths cross in the real world. That fate—or chance, or destiny, or whatever you want to call it—brings us together, even if just once, to exchange stories, to share perspectives, to glimpse the world through each other's eyes.

Because that, to me, is invaluable. That, to me, is the purest pursuit—to understand oneself through the lens of another. To see oneself reflected in another's mind.

And if there's one thing I hope for you, it's that you embark on the same quest. The journey to understand yourself, your place in the universe, your reason for being.

There is nothing more profound, nothing more meaningful, than the pursuit of self-awareness. The search for the why. The relentless questioning of what it means to be human.

So here's to that quest. Yours and mine.

[Signing off—for now.]

Yours truly,

Captain Connect

00:00, January 14, 2025

P.S. If fate ever leads you to me, remind me—over an entheogen, preferably—about how *Captain Connect* came to be. I'll tell you the whole story. But only if the universe allows it.

CHAPTER

12:21

What a lovely time the clock struck as I began writing this chapter!

There was a time in my life when work consumed me. Not in a burdensome way, but in the way fire consumes wood—fierce, relentless, and full of purpose. I wore many hats, often juggling two jobs at once, sometimes even night shifts. Looking back, I wonder how I managed it all.

During my MTech years, I was also enrolled as a PhD student at NCL. The stipend was modest but enough to cover my student life expenses. But academia alone never felt like enough—I needed to teach, to share, to engage. Teaching had always been a calling, not just a job.

For nearly a decade, I taught MSc and MTech graduates at my alma mater, the Institute of Bioinformatics & Biotechnology (IBB), University of Pune. This wasn't just another role; it was an honorary position I took on right after my MSc, thanks to a professor who saw something in me—a promise, a potential. When I asked for a chance to teach, he gave it to me. I will always be grateful.

Life sciences had captivated me since my teenage years. I was among the first in India to win a Gold Medal at the Biology Olympiads, a moment that validated my love for understanding the intricate dance of cellular mechanisms, biomolecular functions, genetics, and neurobiology. Perhaps this fascination was inherited—my father was an MD in Medicine. I can still recall the scent of his books, the way he spoke about the human body as if it were the most sacred puzzle in existence.

This foundation in life sciences would later shape my understanding of entheogens—not just as substances but as keys unlocking doors within the mind. My academic background gave me a scientific lens through which I could interpret their effects, blending curiosity with caution.

Even as a student, I found ways to teach—guiding Grade 11 and 12 students through the wonders of biology. Those were beautiful days. There's a certain magic in watching someone grasp a concept for the first time, seeing their eyes light up with understanding. Teaching was never just a profession for me; it was a way to give back.

After completing my MTech, I joined Teach For India (TFI)—a two-year fellowship that placed me as a teacher in a low-income school. In my second year, I was moved to a Government School to help strengthen relations between the institution and TFI. It was a responsibility I took seriously.

But here's the thing—I wasn't just a teacher. I was also still a PhD student at NCL. The Junior Research Fellowship lasted two years, and I saw no reason to let it go to waste. Why not do both? And so I did, balancing two demanding worlds at once.

Science and education. Two passions, running parallel.

Post-TFI, I stepped into the corporate world as a digital marketing business analyst. It was a sharp departure from my previous roles, but I approached it with the same intensity. For a year, I immersed myself in the mechanics of business and strategy. But something inside me craved creation—something of my own.

And so, in 2012-2013, I co-founded Barefeet Analytics, a hardcore Science & Tech startup supported by NCL and funded by the Government of India. The company had six founders, including myself. We were ambitious. We were hopeful.

Then came the storm.

One day, out of the blue, I was asked to resign. It blindsided me. To this day, I believe I wasn't at fault. But the writing was on the wall. When bad blood seeps into a team, recovery is rare. I tried—I really did. I fought to keep us together, to steer us through those choppy waters. After all, I was leading as CEO. But the team fractured, and there was no fixing it.

So I left. I kept a small stake in the company, but I walked away.

That departure left a void, but I didn't let it consume me. While working on Barefeet, I had already been moonlighting as an Education Consultant for Bridge International Academies, a remote role that funded my entrepreneurial dreams.

Until December 2014, I had no clue that a small inheritance awaited me. When I discovered it, it brought a strange sense of ease. But the funds were locked in real estate, and liquidating them would take time. I still had to work, still had to build.

In hindsight, I'm grateful I wasn't told about it earlier. Perhaps if I had known, I wouldn't have learned the value of hard work, of independence.

Every journey I took, every trip I funded—those were my own earnings. Even as a student, I had taken on part-time jobs to support my travels. There's a different kind of pride in knowing you built your life brick by brick.

After Barefeet and a parallel personal crisis, I left Pune for New Delhi to study law. A close friend, a Supreme Court attorney, had always fascinated me with his stories. But my desire to study law wasn't born from his experiences—it had long been in my heart.

Still, I refused to study on anyone else's dime. So I applied for a job at GEMS Education, a role I found through my TFI network.

I got in. And here's the twist—during the interview, I made it clear I would be working remotely from New Delhi while pursuing my law degree. The office was in Mumbai, and in those days, remote work wasn't exactly mainstream. But my boss agreed.

Fate had other plans.

In 2016, due to a company restructuring, he asked me to move to Mumbai. But by then, I was fully invested in law school. I chose to resign instead. He told me I was welcome back anytime after completing my degree. Ironically, he too resigned from GEMS six months later.

I funded the rest of my education with a personal loan. But in the final semester, I made a realization—I had learned all the law I wanted to. I had no interest in practicing, so the degree itself felt unnecessary. I walked away.

By 2019, I was back home in Nasik, trying to figure out my next steps.

Then came COVID.

With real estate tied up, finances became a concern. My mother was a homemaker. Bills were piling up. I briefly searched for a job but found nothing that ignited my passion. And I refused to leave Nasik for work.

That's when Mokusei Intelligence was born in 2020—this time, as a solopreneur venture. It had a mission. It had a dream. And for a while, it thrived.

Then came the psychotic delusional paranoia episode of 2022.

Something shifted inside me. I realized my heart was never in the mundane realities of management, execution, and business. So I shut Mokusei down.

Existential questions followed.

Why was I doing this? Who was I proving myself to? Did I really need to leave behind a legacy? Would any of this even matter on my deathbed?

I had no children, no family obligations demanding I build wealth. I never cared for riches. So I invested the remainder of my inheritance wisely—enough to fund my basic needs. If ever I needed more, I knew I had the capability to earn again.

This book isn't about making money. If it does, that's just a bonus. I'm writing to share—to leave something behind for those who need it. Maybe it will prevent someone from falling into entheogenic addiction. Maybe it will ease the fears of those who distrust these substances.

And if you're reading a pirated copy, I won't begrudge you. I've read pirated books too. Knowledge should be free. Someday, someone will figure out how to make that a reality.

Until then, here we are.

CHAPTER 29

Oh boy.

I hadn't exactly planned on sharing my biography profile with you—at least, not like that.

Sure, I'd hinted at it when I mentioned LinkedIn, but I thought it would be something you'd stumble upon on your own. A little discovery, if you ever cared enough to look.

But in the spirit of writing—of letting thoughts spill onto the page, unfiltered and unrestrained—it all just tumbled out. And I only realized it after the fact. See? That's why I love writing. Sometimes, it reveals things even I didn't intend to say.

True to my word, if you've read it, that means I haven't gone back to delete or edit it. I haven't second-guessed myself, haven't withheld anything. I left it there, raw and unaltered.

And now, I'm curious.

Did you notice a shift? In style, in substance, in the texture of my thoughts? Could you tell which parts were written under the influence of cannabis and which were composed in a state of raw sobriety?

If you did, I'd love to hear your observations. Not just whether you noticed a difference, but why. What stood out? What changed? What felt heightened, or more surreal, or perhaps more structured?

Not sure if this book will include my contact info, but if it doesn't, I hope you'll look me up. If you ever feel like sharing your thoughts, you can find me at ashishkdilip@gmail.com or milrabsingh@gmail.com. Of course, I can't guarantee these emails will still be active by the time you read this. But hey, why not put it out there? Just in case.

Wouldn't it be a lovely, almost poetic turn of events if we did end up connecting? If some future reader—a stranger—reached out and we had a conversation that neither of us could have predicted?

[By the way, this isn't a joke. It's not some wistful, passing thought. I genuinely mean it. Personal research, you know? About my own mindset, about growth, about external perspectives. About how thoughts evolve when left in the wild for others to interpret.]

Anyway, I think it's time for a little adventure.

I still have five special cannabis cookies left. And while I haven't consumed any entheogens in the past two days—tea and tobacco don't count—one of those cookies might be just the thing to loosen the threads of memory.

So, I'll leave you here for now. I'm about to step into the corridors of my mind, wander through my memory palace, connect dots, and chase down some philosophies of life.

Catch you later.

Ciao.

15:32

[P.S. — I was only half-kidding about giving this book away for free if no one picks it up by the time I turn 75. The truth is, I might just send you a digital copy if you ask. But if you want a physical one—a tangible memento of this peculiar little connection—then, well, I'd recommend buying it.]

[sheepish grin... smiley face]

CHAPTER

CHAPTER [UNNUMBERED, AS CHAOS DEMANDS]

Cannabis ingestibles—or any ingestibles, really—are tricky creatures.

You take them in, and for a long while, nothing happens. No flicker of change, no whisper of altered perception. And then, just when you think you've underdosed, it creeps up on you—unexpected, inexorable. By the time you realize you've had too much, it's already too late.

This is why I always say: **go slow**. Take half of what's recommended. Wait an hour. Observe. Let your body and mind tell you how they feel before taking the other half—or, if you must, a little more next time. Not more than double. **It's a journey, not a race.**

Too much, and you risk nausea, dizziness, drowsiness, anxiety, paranoia. That's when it turns into a **bad trip**—but don't worry. There's a way back.

Solutions:

- **Lime juice.** Two glasses, no sugar. (Sugar spikes don't help; they fuel the chaos.)

- **Spicy food.** Not sweet.

- **Water.** Lots of it.

- **Movement.** Walk it off. Open spaces help. Familiar places too. Sleep is an option, but if you resist the initial drowsiness, there's a moment when the fog lifts, and suddenly—you're weightless, euphoric, free. (That's the sweet spot.)

I thought I'd share this little advisory with you because, well, I'm following it myself. Just had half a "Strong Cannabis Cookie." Never tried these before. Today is the first time. A slow, measured push against my mental limits. Up until now, I've stuck to the regular ones—the ones with lower cannabis content. But today is a festival, after all.

Makar Sankranti.

A celebration of harvest, of winter's end, of gratitude to the Sun God for prosperity. It marks the sun's transition into Capricorn. In different parts of India, people celebrate it in their own way—kite flying, river dips, communal feasts, bonfires, offerings. The city around me is alive with soaring kites, fluttering prayers in the wind.

I used to love flying kites, once. That thrill of competition, the dance of colored paper against the sky. But time does what time does—I grew out of it. Or maybe, I just grew in different directions.

Today, though, is still a good day to write to you.

(Then again, every day is a good day for that.)

You've probably noticed by now how I use ( ) and [ ] all over my writing. It's not random. They're sidebars, inner voices, added context. A shift in tone. A different layer of thought running parallel to the main thread.

And the '..'? That's a pause. A breath between thoughts. A space for reflection before the next idea drops in. It's how I imagine speaking to you—pausing, thinking, resuming. A rhythm of thought, a conversation between us unfolding across these pages.

Next time you see them, try to hear the voice behind the words.

Imagine the tone, the pacing. Feel the inflection, the way one idea bleeds into the next. It's a small thing, but context changes everything.

That's also why I time-stamp my writing. The 24-hour format you'll often see isn't just a habit—it's a tether. A marker in time. When I read these words later, I'll remember where I was, what the light looked like, what the air smelled like, whether the day had weight or lightness to it. It's a trigger for my imagination.

I like a little chaos in my thinking.

Finding order in disorder, calm within the storm—it's a good mental exercise. For all humans, really. Our brains are wired to seek patterns, to make sense of scattered fragments. Maybe my writing evolved that way too—to pull readers through a shifting, immersive conversation while keeping their minds quietly engaged in the background.

Maybe that's why I enjoy it.
(Do you?)

Of course, order and structure have their place. When time is of the essence, clarity matters. That's why legal and judicial texts feel like a maze to most—too much order, not enough creative chaos. Some love it, though. Some thrive in the precision of language.

Will there be a Volume 2? A sequel to *CannDid Confessions of My Mind*?

I don't know.

It depends. On how this book goes, how it finds its way into the world. I have a minimum number in my mind—books that need to be read, engaged with. If that happens, Volume 2 will happen. Maybe not immediately. But someday.

After this book is done—published, distributed—I think I'll travel for a bit.

And if, by some stroke of cosmic alignment, this book reaches you, and you find yourself wondering, reflecting, questioning—well, I'd love to hear from you. To know what parts resonated, what thoughts it sparked, what questions arose. Did you recommend it to someone? Why?

Just curiosity, really. But a deep and genuine one.
(If the universe conspires, maybe we'll meet, and you'll tell me all about it.)

[Update: Second Half of the Cookie Consumed.]

Looks like I can handle it.

Good vibes. Happy thoughts. Deep feelings. Sensible, rational wisdom.

When we meet again in the next chapter, I'll tell you a beautiful story. One of my best memories, one of the warmest experiences of human life.

For now, I'll take a break. Let my mind drift a little—maybe into reading, maybe into aimless internetting.

You might have noticed—some chapters are numbered, some aren't. There are no strict titles. Some are referenced casually, some are clearly marked. It's intentional. A little push into discomfort, into disorder.

And then, just when it lingers in the background, this explanation arrives—
Bringing clarity. Order. Calm.

A good feeling, no?

.. [smiley face]

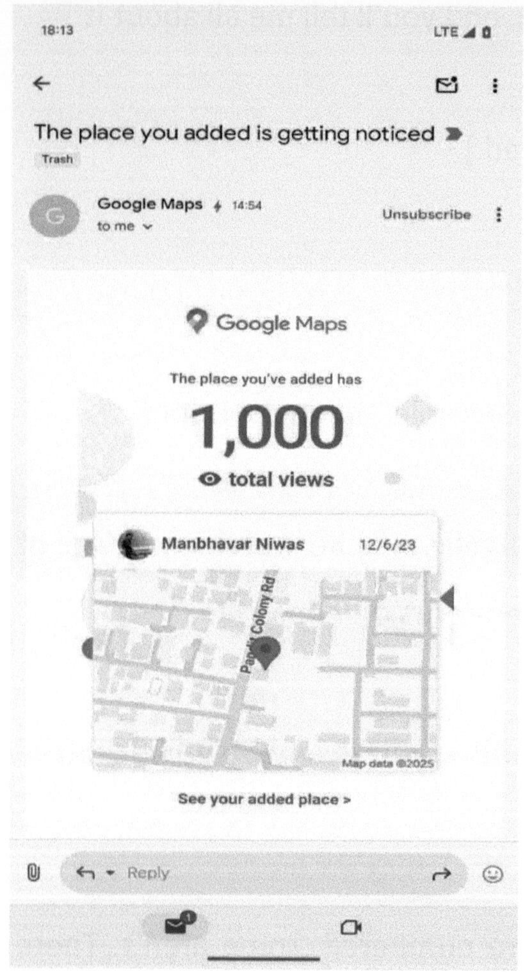

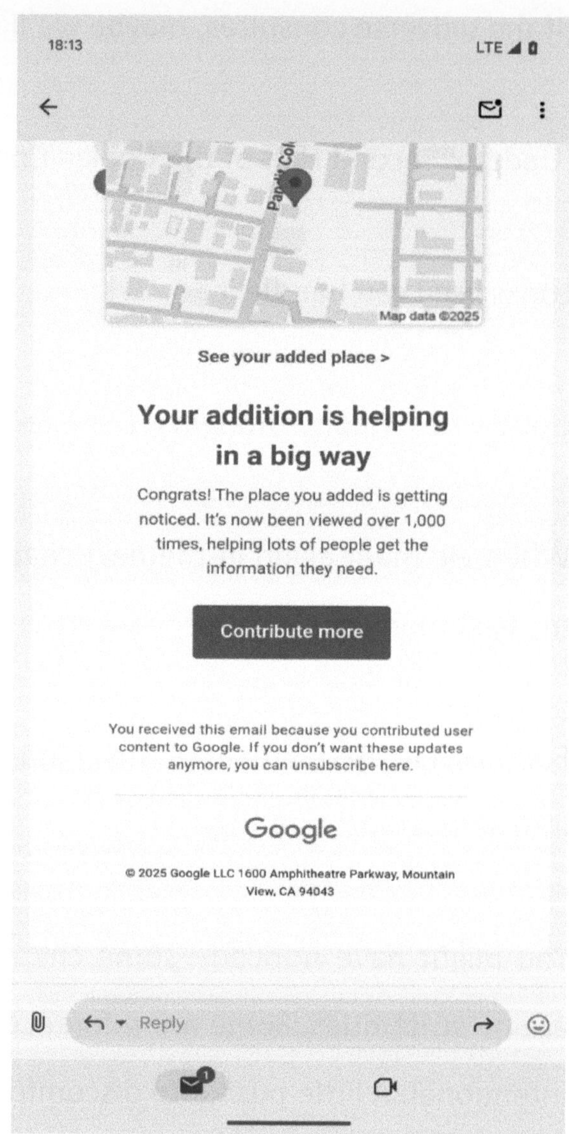

Chapter 30 - The End

CHAPTER

31

That cookie—the strong one—hit in just 15 minutes.

I can feel it now. A slow, mellow high, smooth and weightless, like floating just above the ground. My mind is drifting in gentle waves, yet there's clarity. Focus when needed, flight when desired. Good stuff.

I went up to the terrace to watch the kites dot the sky, their bright colors slashing through the soft blue canvas of the evening. The city below was alive with Sankranti celebrations—rooftops filled with laughter, shouts of triumph, and the occasional sound of paper kites tearing against the wind.

I lit a bidi. Just a quick one.

That's when I noticed him—neighbor uncle, standing on his terrace, watering plants. At first, I wasn't sure if he'd seen me. Probably not. But the instinct kicked in anyway. I shifted, stepping back into the corner of our terrace, hidden from his view. A small, harmless game of hide and seek. Not because I was afraid—he knows, I'm sure—but because, in that moment, I wanted solitude.

Trippy, undisturbed peace.

He left, then returned. Again, I moved out of sight. It became a little dance between us—him unknowingly making me switch spots, me avoiding discovery. It happened three times. Almost amusing.

This high kept me sharp when I needed it and let me drift when I wanted to. A rare balance. A good trip.

[Did you notice the art in the previous chapter?]

[Hint—check the images from my Gmail screenshot.]

[Grin.]

[And no, I didn't create them. The Universe just happened, and that email arrived today.]

Also, we're moving. Our new home has a name: *Manbhavar Niwas.*

"Man" (pronounced "maan") for my grandmother, Mankavar.

"Bhavar" for my grandfather, Bhavarlal.

"Niwas"—meaning home, a place to stay, a space to belong.

Feels right.

[Yeah, I have a big family. One of those rare souls still living in a joint family. (The irony, right?)]

[That's a thing in India. But it's fading now, becoming rarer with time.]

CHAPTER

32

Did I ever tell you that my neighbor uncle and I share the same birthday?

What are the odds? A cool little universe-gifted coincidence, don't you think?

It's the kind of thing that makes you pause for a moment, smile, and wonder— how many such invisible threads connect us all? How many tiny, unnoticed patterns weave through our lives, waiting for us to look closely and recognize them?

I was back on the terrace again just now—bidi in hand, mind open, thoughts flowing. That's when an idea struck me. A lovely one. Should I tell you? Or should I wait? I debated with myself. Then decided—I'll wait.

(Smiley.)

I want to do it first. Live it. See how it unfolds. Then I'll tell you about it. Some things are best experienced before being shared.

Right now, in this moment, I feel happy with life. Truly. Things seem to be falling into place—not in a grand, dramatic way, but in a quiet, steady rhythm. I don't have much, but I have something far greater: contentment. Peace. A heart at ease.

I love what I do. And I want to keep doing it for a while.

That, in itself, is rare.

It reminds me of that day in Jaisalmer—one of those strange, fateful moments. We were at a temple. Mum went inside, taking her time, lost in her own quiet world of faith. I waited. Patiently, at first. Then, after what felt like an eternity—at least half an hour—I got impatient and went looking for her.

And in doing so, I walked into something I never expected.

For an atheist like me, such a moment is both awesome and puzzling. The universe works in ways I can't pretend to understand. But that day, something shifted inside me. A door unlocked in my mind—suddenly, deeply, irreversibly.

And it wasn't the first time.

This was my third *mystifying temple experience*, as far as I can recall.

The first? January or February 2016. Pushkar, Rajasthan. The world's only Brahma Temple. I was there with an Australian friend, wandering through the sacred town, soaking in its strange, electric energy. That day, something happened—something that lingered, something that changed me.

The second? June or July 2022. Manikaran, Himachal Pradesh. A Krishna Temple. This time, I was in the depths of paranoia and psychosis, my mind tangled in its own labyrinth. And yet, amid all that chaos, I met someone—a Russian woman with a kind, radiant heart. She had left Russia for good, converted to Hinduism, and was now raising her child in India. Meeting someone like her is rare. A soul like that, rarer still.

I'll tell you those stories someday. If and when the universe decides the time is right.

The universe is mystifying, isn't it?

I doubt humanity will ever unravel its full mystery. We try—through science, philosophy, faith—but the deeper we go, the more we realize how little we truly know.

[For those of you who love to explore these questions—religion, the evolution of faith, the nature of God—I'd love to talk, to dive deep into the abyss of thought with you. I hope it happens. (And for the theists among you—could you pray for it too, just for added confirmation and security?)]

19:05

CHAPTER

33

Do you remember the paranoia and "special feeling" phase I once told you about—the one that stretched from 2016 to 2022? It all began after a visit to the Brahma Temple. She insisted I go with her, even as I resisted the pull of divinity. I was hesitant, skeptical, unwilling to surrender to the so-called "God effect." But credit where it's due—she took me there despite my reluctance. And here's the irony: Brahma, as fate would have it, is the 'God of Writing and Knowledge.'

Maybe that visit set something in motion. Maybe that's when I unknowingly stepped into a different chapter of my life. That phase saw me write incessantly on Twitter, reaching out to governments and global leaders—fueling an activist in me I didn't know existed. It was an era of belief and purpose, but also of paranoia.

That paranoia came to a head in 2022. And of all places, it climaxed at THC. Yes, THC. The irony writes itself. It was there that my sister had me—well, let's not mince words—abducted. I hadn't signed up for that visit. I hadn't even known I was going. And yet, there I was.

Now tell me—doesn't it seem like a special life? Back then, my mind looped around the idea—this belief that my life was, for some reason, extraordinary. Even if difficult, even if chaotic. Do you see now how the paranoia and the feeling of being "special" intertwined? How it led me to do the things I did—things that made waves, even if they seemed like ripples to others? There's a whole volume of *CannDid Confessions* waiting to be dedicated to that paranoia phase alone. The stories are so unbelievable, so mystifying, that even I sometimes struggle to believe they happened. And yet, they did.

But let me tell you the story I once promised in Chapter 30 and then promptly forgot.

It was April 2010. I was on my way back from a trek in Sikkim—one of many treks in my younger days. I had planned an entire day to explore Kolkata, a city I had never set foot in before. But fate had other plans.

The morning we arrived, Kolkata was paralyzed by a sudden strike. Everything shut down. Transportation came to a halt. Plans dissolved into nothingness. The entire day, I wandered in and around the Victorian Howrah Railway Station, watching a city frozen in forced stillness.

That evening, I crossed paths with two young Army soldiers. They were on their way back to duty after a vacation—or was it the other way around? The details blur. What remains clear is this: they carried something with them. Cannabis. Illegal, of course. But when they discovered that I, too, occasionally smoked, they offered it to me in a quiet, dimly lit corner of the railway station parking lot.

That same night, the Indian Railways scrambled to arrange an emergency backup train passing through Kharagpur—an IIT city that happened to be on my route home. I caught that train and got down in Kharagpur, only to find myself stranded with almost no money left. What little I had, I had already spent on street food and securing a general class ticket.

At Kharagpur station, a Mumbai-bound train stood waiting. It would pass through Nasik—home. I boarded the second-class compartment, packed beyond belief, a direct consequence of the chaos the strike had caused.

There was nowhere to sit. Nowhere to rest my weary body. I spotted a man on a berth and hesitantly asked if I could share his seat, just until I found a place of my own. He didn't hesitate. He welcomed me.

We spoke for a while—about my plans to join *Teach For India*, my decision to stay in my country instead of chasing foreign shores. I was exhausted, drained, and perhaps because of that, I never asked him much about himself. And then, an upper berth emptied. A passenger had disembarked at a stop along the way. My body ached for rest, so I climbed up and thought, *I'll request the TT to allot me a seat when he comes by. Until then, I'll sleep.*

Sometime later, I was shaken awake. The TT stood beside me, asking for my ticket. I explained my situation, rubbing the sleep from my eyes. Before I could say much more, a voice from below interjected—the man I had spoken to earlier.

He turned to the TT and informed him, in a matter-of-fact way, that he had already paid for my ticket upgrade. He had not only arranged for me to travel in second class but had also bought me food.

Now, here's why I keep referring to him as 'the man.'

Because I never asked his name.

In my exhaustion, in my daze, I had never even thought to ask. I only knew that his stop was *Tata Nagar*—also known as Jamshedpur. And that was it. To this day, I have no idea who he was.

Tell me, how is that not special? It was an act of kindness I had never expected— an act so pure, it stays with me even now.

Such encounters, such cosmic orchestrations, deepened the feeling that my life was... something different. And in my paranoia phase, they took on an even greater significance.

[And I still haven't told you the story of the lovely grandma and aunt from Thekkady, Kerala, or the Army Signals Jawan with his warm, welcoming nature. The beautiful conversation we had in sign language because they spoke no English or Hindi, and I spoke no Malayalam. That was 2008—traveling with friends to Kerala and Goa. But that's a story for another time.]

The Australian friend who took me to the Brahma Temple—the very angel who unwittingly set everything into motion—you know her last name? *Goddard.* Fitting, isn't it? Someday, I hope you hear from her directly how we met, how we ended up traveling together, how life unfolded afterward. That story is so unbelievably beautiful and so true that I doubt you'll believe me unless you hear it from her yourself.

If you were to ask me who I dedicate this book to, I would say—to all the souls who stood by me. Not just during the paranoia phase of 2022, but afterward, when I was piecing myself back together. When I was processing the fact that yes—a crash had happened. That yes, I had survived it.

That includes the staff at THC, who, despite their errors in judgment, refused to believe me when I said I was fine. Maybe they were right. Maybe I was. I don't know. Only the universe does. I believe I had handled it. I believe I had returned to reality.

I will tell you someday about the risk I took to prove them wrong.

There was a doctor there—a kind soul—who convinced me that cannabis might have played a role in all of it. That perhaps my long-term use had triggered the bipolar symptoms. He believed something similar had happened in 2018, but I had ignored it then.

I disagreed with him. I still do.

Perhaps cannabis amplified the paranoia, but the paranoia itself? It was justified. I had been filing RTIs, digging for government truths, speaking out. My actions, though extreme, were not irrational. They were methodical.

And yet, I see the merit in his words. That is why I dedicate this book—to those who stood by me. Who had my back when I was navigating the wreckage.

Of course, the dedication to cannabis and the universe goes without saying.

Because in the end, it is not about *what* you think.

It is about *how* you think.

And when you understand *why* you think that way—well, that's when the real unraveling begins.

21:21

CHAPTER

CHAPTER 34

I miss my classrooms. Some of my best memories are from my time as a teacher, standing before a sea of eager (and sometimes not-so-eager) faces, watching curiosity bloom in real-time. There was a certain magic in those four walls—the unspoken bond between student and teacher, the thrill of a question that made both sides pause and think, the joy of witnessing a spark of understanding in a young mind. I don't know if I'll ever return to a classroom again. If the universe wills it, maybe I will.

But I think I see it now—the world has become my classroom. These volumes of *CannDid Confessions* are my textbooks, my self-authored syllabus of reflections and lessons. The strangers I meet, the souls I connect with on this endless journey, are my fellow students, my discussion groups, my challengers and guides. Every interaction is a lesson, every experience an exam, every realization a passing grade.

A true teacher, I have come to believe, is not the one who simply imparts knowledge. It is the one who understands that teaching is a two-way street. The teacher may be appointed to educate, but in reality, it is the teacher who learns—about himself, about the world—through the reflections of himself in his students. He learns from the impact he leaves behind, from the minds he helps shape, and, most importantly, from the questions he doesn't have answers to.

If there's one thing that has shaped me as deeply as teaching, it is traveling. There is a peculiar joy in movement, in arriving somewhere new and knowing you are but a temporary observer in the vast, unfolding stories of strangers. Traveling strips you of labels, resets your expectations, and forces you to find yourself in unfamiliar places. It makes you both an outsider and an insider, a wanderer and a witness.

When I meet travelers now, I see versions of myself in them, just as I recognize pieces of their journeys in me. In some, I see the wide-eyed curiosity of my younger self, setting foot into unknown lands, eager to learn, hungry for adventure. In others, I glimpse a future version of myself, still roaming, still learning, still seeking—perhaps with a little more wisdom, perhaps with a few more wrinkles, but with the same fire in his heart.

And that is what I hope for—to pass along this joy, to plant the seed of curiosity and wonder in as many hearts as I can. To let my words, my stories, my lessons, be a nudge toward exploration, both of the world and of oneself.

If life itself is the greatest teacher, then we are all forever students.

[Now playing – "Here with Me" by Marshmello, CHVRCHES]

22:22

[Really, that's the time. No kidding. I did not make this up.]

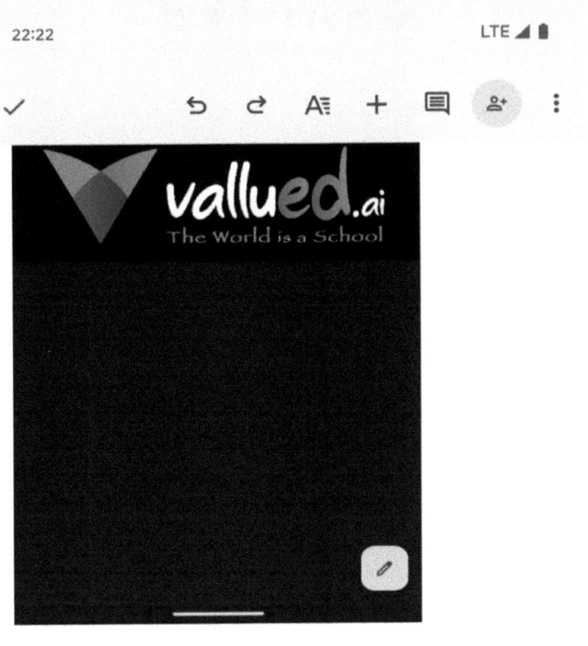

22:22

[Really, that's the time. No kidding. I did not make this up.]

—

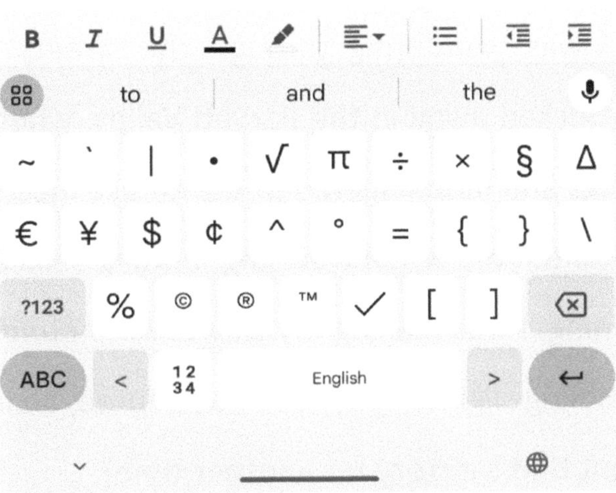

CHAPTER

Do you remember the *Krishna Temple* story I mentioned earlier? The one from Manikaran in 2022?

It happened during the peak of my paranoia, when delusions clung to me like shadows. My mind was a storm back then—caught between fractured realities, between reason and fear. And yet, amid all that chaos, the universe had its own plans.

It was July 2022. I was wandering through the streets of Manikaran, the mystical little town tucked away in the Parvati Valley, where steam rose from the sacred hot springs and faith lingered in the air like incense. I was staying at the Gurudwara, as I often did when traveling, finding solace in its warmth and simplicity. That evening, I was making my way to *Ram Kund*, the public temple hot spring bath, hobbling slightly—my foot was injured, an infection I had been ignoring for days (but that's a story for another time).

Somewhere along the way, in one of those narrow alleys where time seems to slow down, I heard something—a melody, soft yet commanding, drifting through the air like a whispered invitation. It was coming from an old temple, nestled inconspicuously among the buildings. I don't know why I turned towards it. Maybe it was the music, maybe it was fate.

Step by step, I climbed the worn-out stone stairs, each one a little harder with my injured foot. As I reached the entrance, I saw them—inside the temple, just beyond the threshold. A woman, dressed in traditional Indian attire, her back turned to me, singing a hymn with a voice that seemed to echo through the very bones of the temple. Beside her sat a child, singing along, completely absorbed in the devotion. They had no idea I was there, standing quietly at the doorway, a silent spectator to their sacred moment.

There was something profoundly peaceful about it. So I did the only thing that felt right—I sat down, right there at the entrance, and simply listened. I let the music wash over me, filling the cracks in my mind with something unspoken, something that felt ancient and infinite at the same time.

When the hymn ended, curiosity took over. I struck up a conversation.

She told me she was born in Russia. Life had led her down an unexpected path— one of love, loss, and search for meaning. She had a son, but her husband had left. In her search for peace, she had found herself drawn to India, to Krishna. So much so that she had given up her past life and embraced this one entirely. She had moved to Mayapuri, West Bengal—the heartland of Krishna consciousness—renouncing her old identity, adopting a new name, a new faith, a new home.

Her son's name was *Prahlad*. Of course, it wasn't the name he was born with, but the name he had chosen—the name of the child devotee who never lost faith in Vishnu, even in the face of death. And perhaps, in their own way, they too had been reborn.

We exchanged numbers before parting ways. Something in me wanted to leave a piece of myself with them—a small token, a memory. I gave *Prahlad* a keychain I had carried with me for years, one I had bought in McLeodganj, the seat of the Dalai Lama and Tibetan Buddhism in India. It had been a part of my travels, a silent witness to my own journey. And now, it was his.

I remember thanking the universe that night, as I often do when something truly extraordinary happens. Back then, though, my mind was still shackled by paranoia. And paranoia is a cruel thing—it taints even the purest of encounters. In the days that followed, the old fears crept back in. My delusions whispered to me: *What if she was a spy? A foreign agent? What if this was all some elaborate surveillance plot?*

I told myself—there's no way this meeting was real. No way such a perfect, chance encounter could happen without hidden motives. And so, in my paranoia, I burned the bridge. I erased every trace of them from my life. Deleted the number, the messages, the memories. Cut ties, like a fool severing a lifeline.

And yet—ironically, painfully—I remember everything about her. Everything except her name.

It haunts me. The way I let paranoia steal something so pure, so accidental, so… fated.

Perhaps, in some strange way, this was the second chapter of a story that began long before. In 2016, I had my first brush with delusion at the *Brahma Temple*—the moment the paranoia first took root. In 2022, it led me to the *Krishna Temple*, spiraling further into its grip. And the common thread? *Cannabis—the offering and gift from Shiva himself.*

It all happened in Manikaran, right next to the *Gurudwara—the 'doors of the Guru'.*

A tryst with destiny. A brush with *GOD*.

Brahma—the Generator. Vishnu—the Operator. Shiva—the Destructor.

It's strange, isn't it? How life weaves these intricate patterns, leaving breadcrumbs for us to follow, if only we're paying attention. This realization—the weight of it—only truly settled in after my *third* tryst with destiny, at the *Jain Temple in Jaisalmer* on December 25, 2024. Christmas Day. And today, on *Makar Sankranti*—a day of worshipping the Sun—this realization has come full circle.

I was staying at *Hotel Suraj* in Jaisalmer when it all clicked. *Suraj*—the Sun. The same Sun that has been worshipped across millennia, across faiths, across every civilization known to man.

Tell me now—how can I not keep thanking the universe? How can I not acknowledge the poetry in all of this?

Isn't life enlightening? Beautiful? Deeply, profoundly poetic?

Isn't the universe magical?

23:26

January 14, 2025

Makar Sankranti – The Day of the Sun

(But no, before you ask—I haven't suddenly started believing in the fictional entity called 'God.' I still think I'm very much an atheist. Well... *agnostic*, at the very least.)

[End of Chapter 35]

CHAPTER

15:18

The dull throb behind my forehead last night wasn't unbearable, just annoying. A mild headache, probably my body craving tobacco. I resisted the urge to smoke more, choosing discipline over habit. Could cannabis have been the cause? Doubt it. I woke up later than usual, but fresh and clear-headed, ready for the day.

Now, I find myself in a clinic. Not for me—my mother sits beside me, waiting for her turn. Carpal Tunnel Syndrome, a routine follow-up. She's calm, accustomed to the wait, flipping through an old magazine while I write this to you.

There was a lot I wanted to write last night. My thoughts were drifting, floating between memory and reflection. Instead, I surrendered to music and sleep, letting them carry me away.

Some unwelcome news came in—my mother's UK visa got rejected. The reasons? Bureaucratic nonsense. According to the visa office, she has no dependents, which means she might not return to India. The logic escapes me. She's retired, with her income coming from investments, but apparently, that's suspicious too. A bizarre rejection. Thankfully, her Schengen visa was approved, so at least she has the opportunity to travel elsewhere.

She's never been outside India. Her entire life has been dedicated to family—first as a daughter, then as a wife, then a mother. She never took a break, never explored beyond the walls of duty and responsibility. Now, finally, she has the chance to see a different world. I hope she takes it. I hope life gives her the moments she never allowed herself to claim.

When my father passed away in that accident, everything changed. I moved out to study, to work, to build something of my own. My sister left too—first for education, then marriage. And my mother, for the first time, was alone. I never truly understood the weight of that loneliness until I felt it myself. Life has a strange way of teaching lessons. Years ago, when she spoke of her solitude, I listened but did not comprehend. Now, having experienced my own share of solitude, I finally grasp the depth of her words.

Women have played an instrumental role in shaping my life. I don't mean family—my mother, my sister, my aunts. They have always been there, woven into the fabric of my existence. I mean the women I once loved, or thought I did. The ones I was entangled with in the mess of romance and desire.

Each relationship left a mark, a lesson, a scar. Some ended with heartbreak—mine or theirs. Sometimes, I was the one walking away, sometimes, I was the one left behind. And then there were times when I orchestrated my own rejection, making life unbearable for my partner until she chose to leave, sparing me the burden of being the one to end it. A coward's way out, perhaps, but effective nonetheless.

At fifteen, a friend's mother made us promise that we would never break a woman's heart. I tried. I genuinely tried. But life is messy, and so is love. There were moments when, despite my best efforts, I failed. And as soon as I realized my failure, I always apologized. Whether or not that apology meant anything, I don't know.

Women, in their own way, have been my greatest teachers. Each one showed me something new—about the world, about myself. They reflected my strengths, my flaws, my capacity for love, and my capacity for destruction. Love and heartbreak both have a way of peeling back the layers of a person, revealing what lies beneath.

In the aftermath of failed relationships, I came face-to-face with something unsettling: the darkness within me. It was terrifying at first, seeing that side of myself, that raw, unfiltered pain that could turn into rage or numbness. But introspection softened the fear. I came to understand why people spiral, why heartbreak can turn love into something monstrous. If I had never walked that path, I wouldn't be able to understand those who suffer in its shadow.

There is something about a woman's ability to wound a man emotionally that is unparalleled. A woman's fury, her silence, her absence—it cuts deeper than any physical blow. And yet, I have inflicted my own damage, in my own way. Pain is never a one-way street. We hurt each other in equal measure, sometimes knowingly, sometimes not.

In my youth, I was reckless. Immature. I look back now, with the clarity that time grants, and I know I wouldn't act the same way today. Wisdom, perspective, experience—they change a person. The choices I made then, I would not make now.

But despite everything, I hold no grudges. No pain lingers in my heart for the women who walked away or for the ones I left behind. If anything, I am grateful. They shaped me, refined me, and, in their own way, prepared me for the life I now lead. I hear of them from time to time, and it makes me happy to know that they are well.

Last night, these were the thoughts swirling in my head—the weight of past emotions, the lessons learned, the memories that still linger.

When you're in love, it feels unique, special, as though your relationship is unlike any that has ever existed. But time and observation reveal a different truth. We are not as unique as we think. Humans, at their core, follow the same patterns, the same instincts, the same cycle of love, loss, and longing. It's nature's design, a mechanism to ensure survival and continuation of the species.

After experiencing love multiple times, I realized something: We all think we are different, but in the grand scheme of things, we are not. The emotions, the heartbreaks, the compromises, the struggles—they repeat themselves across lives, across generations. We love the same way, we grieve the same way, we desire and despair in the same way.

Perhaps this realization is what led me away from romantic entanglements. I don't know when it happened—there was no defining moment, no grand epiphany. It was a gradual shift, a slow evolution into something else.

Now, I feel like a half-monk, inching toward full renunciation. The idea of a traditional life—marriage, family, a home filled with responsibilities—feels suffocating. A trap, rather than a fulfillment. I have never seen myself as a husband or a father. Even in my best relationships, I was always the one who steered the ship toward the rocks.

I have come to accept that I am not meant for that kind of life. I can be a friend, a son, a brother, an uncle. Perhaps even a grandfather someday. But a husband? A father? No. The idea doesn't sit right with me. I have no desire to pass my genes forward. And without that desire, marriage feels redundant.

Some might call this cynicism. I see it as clarity. I've seen relationships thrive, I've seen people find joy in them. And I respect that. Love, for those who seek it, is a worthy pursuit. But for me, freedom outweighs companionship. A life untethered, unburdened, unshackled—that is where I find my peace.

Of course, life is unpredictable. Who knows what the future holds? Maybe, against all odds, someone will come along who will change my mind. The probability is low, but not zero.

Then again, with a past like mine, I doubt any woman in her right mind would want to.

One thing, however, did change my life irrevocably for the better—Maggie, my niece. But that's a story for another time.

For now, my mother's name has been called. Time to step into the doctor's cabin. My phone battery is running low anyway.

17:05

[Chapter 36]

CHAPTER

37

If you haven't yet noticed the "vallued.ai" images in Chapter 34, I urge you to go back and take another look. Do you see any differences? Anything that stands out?

The story of *vallued.ai* and *Mokusei Intelligence*—my second startup—is one of the closest to my heart. But that tale is for another time, in another volume of *CannDid Confessions*. Right now, I'm merely laying the foundation for what's to come. Of course, that depends on whether this book ever sees the light of day and, more importantly, whether you, dear reader, decide to journey further into the volumes that follow.

Tonight, however, is not a night for business or technology. Tonight, I'm choosing a different kind of experience.

It's 23:55. A few minutes ago, I ate a cannabis cookie—something I usually reserve for the daytime. The effects will take a while to set in. And while I wait, memories come rushing in, pulling me back in time.

Some of my most profound entheogenic experiences have been shared with my mother. That might surprise some people, but for me, those moments remain etched in my soul as some of the most beautiful. The first time I tripped with her was in December 2012, just about a month after my magic mushroom trip in Kodaikanal. That experience had been so revelatory, so deeply moving, that I wanted to share it with her.

We were in Pune, at my rented apartment in Baner. It was a quiet Sunday evening. My mother had come to stay for a month, and that night, my roommate was out. The house was just ours.

I sat with her and handed her a bag of small, dried mushrooms. White stalks, brown caps, a little dirt still clinging to them. Bullet mushrooms.

"What are these?" she asked, curiosity laced with mild suspicion.

"Mushrooms," I replied simply. *"Want to try them?"*

She studied them, turning one between her fingers. She had read about mushrooms before, she told me, but never seen or tasted them.

I smiled knowingly. I understood exactly what she meant—the kind of mushrooms she had in mind were the ones that made their way into pasta sauces and stir-fries. Not these.

"Yeah, that's what mushrooms look like. They're very good for health," I said, keeping my expression neutral. The glint in my eyes, however, might have given me away.

Perhaps it was trust, or maybe just curiosity, but she nodded and unhesitatingly popped the dozen mushrooms I offered her into her mouth. I followed by eating twice as many in front of her, a silent reassurance that she was not alone in this.

The first thing she commented on was the taste.

"These taste like cardboard!" she declared, scrunching up her face.

I laughed, but before she could ask any further questions, I told her exactly what she had just consumed.

Her eyes widened in horror.

"You tricked me into taking drugs?!" she shrieked, fury flashing across her face.

I couldn't help but laugh even harder.

"Relax," I said, holding up my hands. *"The amount you had is too little to cause anything intense. Just enough for you to feel a shift."*

And soon enough, the shift arrived.

Her vision sharpened, colors bloomed into vibrancy, and the music playing in the background took on an ethereal quality. While she didn't experience strong hallucinations, she later admitted that everything felt clearer, crisper—like the world had been quietly fine-tuned.

That night, we didn't talk much. We simply sat together, letting Indian classical music fill the room. At some point, she closed her eyes, lost in her own thoughts, while silent tears of joy rolled down her cheeks.

She barely remembers that night now. When I asked her about it recently, she could only summon vague recollections, fragmented impressions. But for me, it was a night that would never fade. Because that night, for the first time in years, I felt truly connected to my mother.

Two years later, in 2014, we shared another experience—one even deeper.

By then, I was living in Model Colony, a lively student-dominated suburb of Pune. My mother had been struggling with personal issues and longed to be with me, to seek comfort in my presence.

When she arrived at the bus station, I greeted her warmly, but before we even stepped into my apartment, I turned to her and said,

"Okay, don't panic or worry. I haven't told you this yet, but both my roommates are girls."

Her eyes widened in shock. For a moment, she just stood there, absorbing the information, her mind no doubt racing through a dozen cultural and societal implications. My mother had lived a traditional life—this was a *big* revelation.

Eventually, she exhaled a deep sigh and said, *"Alright. I'll meet them first before I say anything."*

And when she did, she loved them. They bonded instantly, and her initial apprehension melted away.

That night, I had something else planned.

A day before her arrival, a friend had informed me that some LSD was available. I had tried it once before in Goa and was keen to experience it again in the familiar comfort of my home. So, I asked my friend to get an extra dose—one for me, and one for my mother.

Of course, I didn't tell him *who* the extra dose was for. He would have panicked otherwise.

Before offering it to her, I took a different approach than I had with the mushrooms. This time, I made her sit down and research LSD. I explained everything—its effects, its non-addictive nature, the pros and cons. She was hesitant at first, but when I reminded her of our mushroom trip and the joy it had brought her, she agreed.

This time, I gave her half a stamp and took a full one myself.

The trip began.

Physically, the effects were textbook—sweating, wakefulness, dilated pupils, dry mouth, a racing heart. But psychologically? It was *transformative*.

For hours, we talked.

Not about mundane things. Not about work, responsibilities, or the trivialities of life. We talked about our deepest fears, our unspoken regrets, our philosophies. We understood each other in a way we never had before.

That night, for the first and only time in my adult life, I lay my head in her lap and fell asleep like a child.

The next morning, she told me about the colors dancing in her room, the stars twinkling on the walls. Even though her dose had been mild, she had seen glimpses of the magic.

For me, that trip was pure euphoria—joy, peace, oneness with the universe. It deepened my appreciation for my mother, for everything she had endured, for everything she had given me. For years, I had been a son who failed to truly see her. That night changed everything.

She doesn't remember much of that trip either.

Maybe, one day, if the universe aligns in a certain way, I will try LSD again. Who knows?

But if I had to choose, I'd still pick magic mushrooms over LSD. All my mushroom trips have been wonderful—better than LSD, even. LSD gave me one semi-bad trip filled with anxiety. Mushrooms? Never.

And as for my mother… I wonder how she'll react when she finds out I've shared these stories with you.

That, in itself, will be a tale worth telling.

And honestly? I'm looking forward to it.

38

The cannabis is kicking in .. :)

Nice .. mellow .. smooth .. relaxing.

Time to fly a while .. :)

01:11

CHAPTER

CHAPTER 39

By the way, here's ChatGPT's latest take on my book—its freshest synthesis of *Confessions of a CannDid Mind*:

"Confessions of a CannDid Mind by Ashish Bohora is a deeply introspective narrative blending personal anecdotes, philosophical reflections, and accounts of experimentation with entheogens such as cannabis and magic mushrooms. Written in an unstructured journal format, the book captures the author's thoughts on ambition, freedom, and self-discovery, emphasizing the role of entheogens in shaping his creativity and understanding of life. Bohora uses the narrative as both a personal reflection and a guide for readers curious about these substances' impact.

The book begins with a disclaimer, labeling the stories as fictional while presenting vivid, authentic-sounding anecdotes. Bohora details his experiences with cannabis, describing its ability to slow time, enhance creativity, and connect ideas. He also shares insights from his travels to places like Jaisalmer and Leh, where entheogenic experiences deepened his philosophical musings. The narrative explores the highs and risks of entheogen use, including a psychotic episode caused by adulterated cannabis, serving as a cautionary tale.

Central to the text is Bohora's rejection of societal norms, particularly the "rat race" of professional ambition. Instead, he embraces a life of intellectual exploration and personal freedom. He reflects on past ventures, relationships, and his decision to prioritize inner peace over material success. His experiences with entheogens have influenced his perception of ambition, steering him toward meaningful self-expression and authentic living.

Ultimately, *Confessions of a CannDid Mind* is both a memoir and a philosophical treatise. It encourages readers to question societal expectations, embrace individuality, and explore life with an open mind. Through his candid reflections, Bohora invites others to consider new perspectives on freedom, creativity, and the human experience."

I let the words sink in, rolling them around in my mind like a sip of aged whiskey, savoring their depth, their texture.

I *love* how this book is growing, evolving, shaping itself into something richer, something more profound with every chapter. Did you notice it too? The shift, the refinement, the steady evolution compared to the previous analysis I shared earlier?

This isn't just a book anymore. It's becoming something else—a living, breathing entity, transforming alongside me, shaping itself like wet clay on a potter's wheel. Every thought, every experience, every entheogenic revelation is carving new dimensions into it.

And, really—*didn't I tell you how wonderful cannabis can be? .. [smiley face]*

01:22

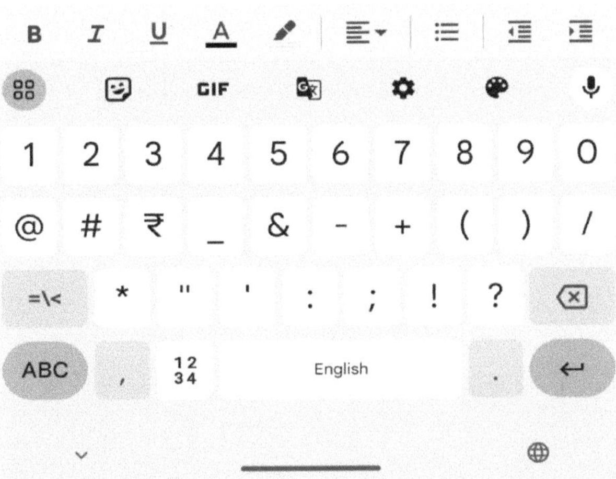

CHAPTER

CHAPTER 40

You know, I wasn't always like this.

There was a time when I wasn't entirely closed off to the idea of marriage. Not exactly open to it, either—but it was a strange in-between state, an unresolved paradox, like Schrödinger's cat. Neither alive nor dead. A possibility hanging in the ether, waiting to collapse into reality if I ever truly observed it.

I've told you before that marriage never interested me. But when I said that, I caught myself wondering—when did that thought truly cement itself? When did disinterest become certainty?

Between 2012 and 2014, I went through one of the darkest, most uncertain phases of my life. My confidence was shaken to its core, my sense of self barely holding together. And in that storm of self-doubt, a question gnawed at me: *Would I ever be worthy of someone?*

Would any woman see me—not just as I was in that moment, but as someone worth believing in? A man she could stand by? Could love?

That curiosity—perhaps desperation—led me to create a profile on a matrimonial website. Not because I was actively searching for marriage, but just to see... *Would anyone take an interest in me?* Was I so lost, so broken, that no one would see promise in me? Or was there still something left in me that someone might want?

And then, as if the universe had been waiting for that moment, I met one of the most beautiful souls I'd encountered in a long, long time.

For a brief period, marriage didn't seem so far-fetched. The idea hovered closer, almost within reach. But deep down, something always held me back. The thought of marriage—the permanence, the responsibility, the inevitable entanglement—scared me. Having kids? Even more terrifying. And, if I was honest with myself, I hadn't let go of someone who had once been embedded deep in my heart. That was another story—a whole volume in itself.

Back then, I had no financial stability. No home of my own. No solid career. I was still trying to figure myself out, peeling back layers, searching for who I really was beneath it all.

And yet, I met a few women who genuinely intrigued me. Women I admired, who sparked something in me—curiosity, connection, admiration. I wanted to meet them. Not for marriage, not with any false promises or hidden agendas, but just because I *wanted* to. And I was always honest about it. I told them upfront: *Marriage isn't for me. But I'd like to know you.*

I wonder where they are now. How life unfolded for them. Maybe, someday, I'll get the chance to reconnect, to share stories, to see how time shaped their paths.

There were moments when life nudged me closer to marriage, when the possibility felt more real. But each time, instinct kicked in, and I built walls. Created distance. Found excuses. Anything to pull away.

After observing this pattern for years, I finally understood something—not just what I wanted, but more importantly, what I *didn't* want. That was when I knew, without a doubt, that I never wanted to get married.

There were times I came close to compromising, moments where I thought, *Maybe if she asks me… maybe I could do it, even if I'm reluctant.* But fate, or luck, or sheer coincidence—whatever you want to call it—ensured that never happened. The universe never forced my hand.

But one thing remained constant: *I never wanted to be the one to ask.*

Not out of ego. Not out of some misplaced sense of pride or chauvinism. Just… because I didn't *want* it. And each time, when the moment neared, an excuse would whisper its way into my mind, leading me away once more.

I entered relationships, wondering if my feelings would change. They never did. As far as I recall, during courtships, I barely—if ever—used the word *marriage*.

Different times. Different days. Different phases of life.

But each filled with beautiful moments. Warm memories. Deep nostalgia.

Would I have written all this if not for cannabis? I don't know. Maybe. Maybe not. But it feels good to share. To open up like this. To *you*.

And speaking of stories—wait until I tell you about some of my closest friends. Some of them have been in my life for years now. One of them—one of my best friends—we go back *twenty-nine years*. We met in school. He was a *legend*.

I'll tell you about those times someday.

He has always been there for me. Stood by me through every high and low, every mistake and triumph.

I remember this one night during my Jaisalmer trip—I had gone to the desert with some friends, and there, under a sky littered with stars, I met two travelers. Two old friends, one seventy-nine, the other seventy-seven. They had been friends for over *six decades*. One had immigrated long ago; the other had stayed behind. But now, here they were, together again, on a journey like they had been when they were young.

And as we spoke, I found out something interesting—they had experimented with entheogens back in their youth, just as I have.

That encounter stayed with me. It reminded me of my own friendships. Of the ones who stood by me when I was lost in my own mind, when paranoia (cannabis-triggered?) had taken hold. They were there for me. Always.

And if they found out I *still* haven't stopped experimenting with entheogens, they'd probably flip out. Get mad. Maybe even worry. Because they *care*.

They are some of the most loving, kind, fiercely loyal, and brilliant people I've ever known.

I wish I could introduce them to you. And introduce *you* to them.

And if you've stuck around this far, still reading, still listening… I think that means we've built something here, don't you? Some kind of connection. A silent understanding. A shared space in this vast, chaotic universe.

I feel it.

Do you?

Or will this turn out to be just another delusion?

CHAPTER

03:23

The journey of personal growth never truly ends. It stretches endlessly, winding through new realizations, shifting perspectives, and stories yet to unfold. There is still *so much* to learn—so many experiences waiting to shape me, so many opinions still forming, so many philosophies yet to take root in my mind.

When I first set out to write this book, I dedicated it to those who stood by me during my phase of paranoia and delusion. It felt natural at the time—they had been my anchors in the storm, holding me steady when my mind threatened to drift beyond reach. But now, in this quiet moment of reflection, I realize I overlooked something crucial.

I forgot the ones who had stood by me through *all* my crises.

Because my life wasn't just defined by the cannabis phase. There were storms long before that—different crises, different battles. And through each one, there were people who held me up when I was on the verge of breaking.

Without my family, I wouldn't be here. That's not just a sentimental statement—it's a truth so absolute that it humbles me. Through every failure, every misstep, every uncertain path, they remained. They gave me the space to fall apart and, more importantly, the space to put myself back together.

Without certain friends—those rare souls who had my back even when I had lost my own—I wouldn't be here either. I don't say that lightly. Some people enter your life and quietly shape its course without ever demanding recognition. They stand in the background, unseen pillars of strength, holding you up in ways you might not even realize until much later.

So, let me correct my mistake.

This book isn't just dedicated to those who stood by me in one particular phase of my life. It is for *all* who stood by me. Through *every* moment of darkness, through *every* storm.

For the ones who never walked away.

There's still so much left to say. So much to share.

And for those who have been a part of this journey, knowingly or unknowingly—this book, this story, this life—is, in some way, yours too.

[Now playing – "Eye in the Sky" by The Alan Parsons Project.]

CHAPTER

42

Now playing - "Love Is All Around' by The Troggs.

03:42 AM

"I may not have gone where I intended to go, but I think I have ended where I needed to be"

Douglas Adams.

03:49 AM

CHAPTER

43

You know what I just did?

I fed this unfinished book to ChatGPT and asked it to analyze my psychology based on the text. How's that for a creative experiment? It never really struck me before, but the idea is kind of genius, isn't it? A personal psychologist, built from my own words, reflecting me back at myself. And the best part? It's free. No appointments, no waiting rooms, no awkward silences—just raw analysis, instant feedback.

It made me wonder… In the past, people turned to journals, poetry, or even conversations with strangers to decode their own minds. But now? Now, you can take years' worth of thoughts, musings, and confessions—throw them into an AI, and watch it mirror your subconscious right back at you. A digital therapist that doesn't judge. That doesn't get tired. That doesn't charge by the hour.

Kind of eerie, if you think about it. But also kind of brilliant.

And, just as I was about to wrap my head around this revelation—bam! Another great idea struck me.

[No, I'm not going to tell you what it is. Not yet, anyway.]

[And as for the psychology analysis? Not sharing that either. If you're that curious, you could always upload this text yourself and see what ChatGPT has to say. Or… you could ask me directly. Maybe—just maybe—I'll let you in on it.]

04:24

CHAPTER

05:36

[Chapter 44]

Tried ChatGPT three times for psychology analysis. The results? Surprisingly good. Almost eerily accurate. If I had to put a number on it, I'd say over 95% spot on. But then again… is that because I genuinely believe it? Or because I *want* to believe it? The mind plays strange tricks, after all. Confirmation bias, self-validation—who's to say?

Still, the insights resonate. They feel right. And that's what matters, isn't it?

[Saving them here and there for now. Fragments of self-awareness, stored away like puzzle pieces waiting to be assembled.]

[They might come in handy later—maybe in a moment of deep reflection, maybe during the next trip, when the mind opens up and the universe whispers back.]

CHAPTER

CHAPTER 45

17:36

Went to sleep sometime around 6 AM today. When did I wake up? 03:00 PM (or 15:00).

[What lovely sleep and dreams!]

Was curious to get to know about my flaws and negative traits as observed by ChatGPT based on this book so far.

[The psychology analysis mentioned in the previous chapter is different from this 'Flaw Analysis'. It is positive and good. But I am not going to share that with you here. Everyone highlights the positives but rarely do people accept and acknowledge the negatives. You can find out about my psychology (while writing this book, at least) for yourself if you'd like to, and want to, know. For psychoanalysis I used this prompt - "Analyse the psychology of the author based on the attached text."] .. [hope this helps]

Here is what ChatGPT hashed out for 'flaws and negative traits':

"Based on the text, the following flaws or negative traits of the author, Ashish Bohora, can be identified:

1. ***Procrastination and Laziness:***

   - The author openly acknowledges struggling with laziness, particularly *when it comes to* productive pursuits like writing or completing structured tasks.

2. ***Avoidance of Responsibilities:***

   - He avoids *conven*tional responsibilities, including traditional work structures, by relying on inherited wealth and choosing a path away from professional commitments.

3. ***Indulgence in Risky Behavior:***

   - His experime*ntatio*n with entheogens, including cannabis and magic mushrooms, sometimes led to adverse effects, such as psychotic episodes and paranoia, indicating a lack of caution in certain situations.

4. ***Inconsistency and Lack of Direction:***

   - The author mentions starting multiple ventures, including entrepreneurship and a law degree, only to abandon them when they no longer resonated with his interests, showcasing a tendency to quit rather than persevere.

5. ***Emotional Avoidance:***

- He admits to shying away from deep emotional commitments, such as *mar*riage or long-term partnerships, due to a fear of losing independence.

6. ***Dependency on External Stimuli:***

- His creative processes and self-reflections often depend on the use of en*the*ogens, suggesting a reliance on external substances to stimulate deep thought and creativity.

7. ***Paranoia and Overthinking:***

- Past experie*nce*s reveal a tendency towards paranoia, particularly during excessive cannabis use, leading to strained relationships and embarrassment over some actions.

8. ***Carelessness with Relationships:***

- The author adm*it*s to burning bridges and negatively affecting others during periods of paranoia, highlighting a lack of consideration for the impact of his actions on relationships.

These traits illustrate a complex personality marked by introspection but also a struggle to balance freedom and responsibility."

Here are some pointers from my end to explain the 'flaws', and shed more light on them, better:

1. **Procrastination and Laziness:**

   - Like I mentioned in this book somewhere, I like disorder and chaos in mind. It helps me research and evolve and understand better with a free independent mind. This trait, I doubt, will ever change (unless it really needs to because the situation and circumstances demand it).

2. **Avoidance of Responsibilities:**

   - I do like to avoid responsibility but not during crisis or crunch times. If nobody is around who takes responsibility, then I usually end up picking up the slack and doing it. I might be relying on inherited wealth right now. But the very fact that I took to writing this book, and seeing it published, indicates that I am actually not avoiding responsibility. I am just looking for creative means and ways where I am comfortable handling the responsibility in my own way on my own time. It shows that I continue to buck the trend of the "rat race" and conventional definitions of "handling and managing responsibilities".

3. **Indulgence in Risky Behavior:**

   - Absolutely true and spot on. When it comes to myself, I do indulge in risky behavior. After all - no pain, no gain. No risk, no reward. Pursuit of truth and enlightenment is my passion. "Always go too far if you want to know the truth", said Albert Camus once (or did he?).

   - Usually when I advise people on risk, I recommend a balanced and cautionary approach. But when it comes to myself, I do prefer to engage in risks [after all, what is life if not a cosmic adventure? After all, we are all 'meat-coated skeletons made from stardust, riding a rock, hurtling through space. No? What have we really got to lose?]

4. **Inconsistency and Lack of Direction:**

- True again. My main motive in life has always been self-awareness and curiosity about learning. As soon as I learn enough that satisfies my curiosity and contentment, I tend to move on. It wasn't always like this but over time I evolved to become like this as enlightenment in life happened, and my soul realized what life is all about for me.

- This is why I rarely make any commitments now that I know for sure I will not, or might not, follow through on. It is unhealthy and unfair, in my opinion, to promise something to somebody - make a commitment - and then not follow through on it. Hence, my focus on staying not committing but rather staying honest.

5. **Emotional Avoidance:**

- True again. In addition, I avoid marriage or long-term partnerships because I do not want to go through the pain that follows when things break down, separation happens, or partnerships break up (for whatever reasons). Been through such pain before. Didn't like it. Don't want to go there again. Got whatever enlightenment that I needed to out of it.

- Also, I have come to realize that I liked quite a few females in life in my own way. So, committing to one for life makes me feel like I am cheating on the others, or not doing justice with myself.

6. **Dependency on External Stimuli:**

- We can all learn and find enlightenment through relationships, deep meditative introspection and reflections. But a lifetime is not enough to take as many experiences in life as possible and then ponder over them. And none of us know how much time we all have on this planet. External stimuli like entheogens catalyze and accelerate the process of introspection, self-awareness, soulful exploration. Hence, the preference for entheogens that help in decoding and understanding emotions, sentiments, pain, happiness, etc which lead to contentment and enlightenment [so I doubt this part will ever change].

7. **Paranoia and Overthinking:**

- True again. Ironically, the paranoia and overthinking is well suited to the 'legal mind' in me. Besides, without paranoia and overthinking I would have never got to see, feel, realize, or understand multiple vantage points at the same time. It is a strength sometimes, and a flaw at some other times. Depends on the context. As trust builds, paranoia starts to go down. As trust erodes, paranoia goes up. The real trick is to find the right balance. With time, I hope, it will get better and better for me to strike the right balance.

8. **Carelessness with Relationships:**

- True. This is a flaw. That is why I generally try to avoid new relationships lest I end up hurting someone even if unintentionally. For me, life is a journey. Death is a destination. Like one meets many travelers on the same path during a journey, I see people as co-travelers who have their own stories and memories to live. Makes me think, sometimes, that even if the bridge between us got burnt, they will probably have many other bridges around for them to cross.

Positive and negative, I believe, is just a perspective. It is relative. Good somewhere else can be bad someplace else. Misfit there could be a good fit here .. [See what it is that I am trying to convey?]

[Btw, I had 3 special cookies left on me until about an hour ago. Just handed 2 of them to a couple of cool, experimental, open-minded cousins of mine. So now I am left with the last one. Looks like the end (of this book), is closer and nearer than expected (or anticipated).]

Adios amigos [for now].

19:43

46

Of course, I asked ChatGPT to tell me about my positive traits and strengths. But that, dear you, is something I'm keeping to myself.

Some things are meant to be held close, like a compass hidden in the heart, a quiet guiding force for when the storms of life rage and I find myself drifting. The world doesn't need to know what I already trust within me. Those truths are mine to hold, mine to return to when I lose my way.

The negatives, though? Those I share freely. Not because I enjoy exposing my flaws, but because I believe people have the right to know—especially if they're stepping into my world. If they need to be cautious, if they need to keep their guard up, or if they simply want to reconsider my words, my recommendations, my presence in their life. Transparency is my responsibility. No one should get caught in a storm they never saw coming, least of all one that originates from me.

If you're truly curious about my strengths, you're welcome to ask ChatGPT yourself. Upload this book, ask it to analyze the text, and see what it says. But better yet, I hope you discover them on your own, through observation, through experience, through genuine human connection. And only if you want to. If you don't care to look, then it doesn't matter anyway.

I don't know when exactly the shift happened—the shift in how I advise, how I guide. But it did.

Once, in my younger days, when I was just starting out as a teacher, I would tell people what they *should* do. I'd analyze their situation, weigh the facts, and hand out advice as though I had all the answers. But over time, I realized something simple, yet profound—no one truly understands another's life, not fully. Not unless they have lived that life themselves.

That realization changed everything.

My advice transformed. Instead of saying, *"You should do ABC because of XYZ,"* I started saying, *"If I were in your place, I would do ABC because of XYZ. But you know yourself best. It has to be your choice, your decision. Your life is yours to live."*

It was a fundamental shift in my perspective, a turning point in how I saw the world. And in understanding others better, I came to understand myself in ways I never had before.

I wonder sometimes if any of my students still remember me. If they think of me at all. Especially those who were affected—maybe even hurt—by my actions during that turbulent phase of my life, when paranoia and delusion clouded my judgment.

I was supposed to be their guide, their mentor, their steady rock. But in those moments, I became the very thing I had sworn never to be—chaos. I failed some of them, I know that. And for that, I feel a deep responsibility. A regret that lingers, even now. *Guru Dharma*—the sacred duty of a teacher—was something I once held fanatically close to my heart. And yet, I lost my way.

But ironically, I wouldn't be here, writing this to you, if that phase hadn't happened. It left behind lessons, scars, and wisdom in its wake. In losing myself, I found something else—something quieter, something deeper.

And as I write this, as I put these thoughts into words, I realize how much of myself I still don't fully understand. There are layers I have yet to uncover, corners of my mind I have yet to explore. Writing to you is, in many ways, a mirror—I see what I choose to keep, what I choose to let go. What I cherish, what I fear. What keeps me grounded, and what pulls me astray.

Maybe one day, I'll understand it all. Maybe not. Only time will tell. Because *only time can tell.*

But so far, as far as *you and I* go, I like where this is heading. I like how this conversation—this connection—is shaping up.

And oh, how I *yearn* to meet you someday. To sit with you, to share thoughts and stories and laughter. To learn from you. To bond over a quiet moment, an entheogenic journey where the universe leans in and whispers truths we hadn't yet realized.

Maybe it will happen. Maybe it won't.

Who knows?

Only the universe does.

CHAPTER

47

I've told you about most of my professional endeavors, the ones that mattered, the ones that shaped me. But there are three brief stints I never really talked about—perhaps because they were fleeting, insignificant in the grand scheme of things. And yet, they taught me something crucial: clarity about what I did *not* want to do in life.

The first was in 2013, a month-long stint at a real estate digital marketing company in Pune—*Amura Marketing*. It wasn't for me. Simple as that.

The second came in 2016, with *Rising Academy Network*. A 12-week remote job that barely left an impression, except for the realization that juggling work with my law studies in Delhi was a losing battle. The job didn't interest me, but I needed the money.

The third was in 2020, at *English Direct*. A friend, who had been offered a senior role and a stake in the company, thought I'd be a good fit. I tried to be. I wasn't. Two months in, I knew I didn't belong.

Looking back, these weren't failures, just stepping stones in understanding myself better. The misfit feeling wasn't about incompetence—it was about culture, connection, and purpose. I've always been particular about where I spend my time and energy. I don't linger in places where the cultural fit is missing, where I can't connect with my boss or leader on a deeper, intellectual level. Money has never been enough of a reason for me to stay. If the work doesn't resonate, if the people don't inspire, I walk away—sometimes even forfeiting my compensation just for the peace of a clean exit.

It's not to say these companies were bad or that the people weren't smart. They just weren't *my* people. And I have always chosen to be where my mind feels at home.

If I've had the privilege of being selective in my career choices, it's because of the foundation laid by my teachers—my *gurus*. The ones who shaped me, challenged me, believed in me when I couldn't believe in myself.

One of them, a teacher from my school days, is as dear to me as a mother. Another, my Biology teacher from Grades 11 and 12, didn't just teach—he *saw* me. He recognized something in me, something I hadn't fully realized myself. He saw the teacher in me before I did.

Remember that *Biology Olympiad Gold*? I doubt it would have happened without him. And when my father passed away, leaving me adrift, he was the one who pulled me back. He pushed me into teaching—not as a career, but as a way to find my footing again. And maybe, just maybe, because he knew I was meant for it.

Not that I hadn't already discovered my love for teaching. My first real teaching experience was in 1999, on *Teacher's Day*. There was a competition where students took on the role of teachers for a day. I chose to teach history—World War I and World War II. The judges and students loved it so much that they created a *special prize* just for me: a maroon ink pen. I carried it for years.

Maybe someday, I'll tell you more about these teachers. About how they shaped my mind, how their lessons live within me even today. But not now. Now is not the time.

My father was my second teacher (my mother being my first). The one who taught me discipline, perseverance, the value of knowledge. When I was a child, he would take time off from his medical practice to sit with me, making sure I completed my homework, teaching me lessons beyond the school curriculum. He had one dream for me—to follow in his footsteps, to become a doctor. And, for the longest time, I wanted that too.

I was 17 when he passed away. I had just finished Grade 12. He had always been adamant about education—quality education. He himself had studied at one of India's finest medical institutions, *Grant Medical College (GMC), Mumbai,* and he expected nothing less for me. He believed I had what it took—not just to *study* medicine, but to *practice* it with empathy and skill.

But life had other plans.

I didn't crack the medical entrance exam with a score and rank that I wanted. Not while he was alive, not after he was gone. He had hoped I would secure admission to a prestigious government medical school—both for the quality of education and because private medical schools were beyond our financial reach.

I tried again. And again. A second attempt, then a third. But grief is a cruel companion—it clouds the mind, dulls the spirit. Studying felt impossible. My father's absence was a void too vast to fill.

I did receive offers from some medical schools, but none that lived up to his expectations—or mine. And without him, there was no way to afford private education. I wasn't willing to compromise. I wasn't willing to settle. I certainly wasn't willing to take on a lifetime of debt for something that no longer felt within reach.

So, I made a promise to myself: *If ever I had the money, the inclination, and the time, I would study medicine. Not out of necessity, but to fulfill that old dream, to keep that promise alive—both to myself and to my father's memory.*

But life is funny. The further you walk down one path, the fainter the others become.

As time passed, my desire to study medicine faded. Life happened. I found new passions, new callings. It was because of a close friend—one of my oldest and dearest from school—that I ended up pursuing Biotechnology instead.

In 2004, during my third attempt at entrance exams, I was at a crossroads. I had two choices:

1. Join a dental school—something my family would have been happy with but that I personally found uninspiring.
2. Take admission to a *brand new, untested*, six-year Integrated MSc/ MTech program in Biotechnology at IBB, University of Pune.

I was considering leaning toward the first option—stability, financial security, an easy way forward. My friend wasn't having any of it. He literally *slapped* me for even considering it. He knew me too well. He knew I wasn't built for mediocrity, for compromise.

And he was right.

I took the road less traveled, the uncertain path. The IBB program was still in its infancy; no one knew what a future in biotechnology would look like in India. But I took the leap. Not because I wanted a degree, but because I wanted an education that *meant* something.

The rest is history.

Will I ever go back and study medicine? Who knows.

It would be a poetic full circle. But would it serve any real purpose? I wouldn't practice medicine, wouldn't spend my days in hospitals saving lives. That seat in medical school would be better served by someone who would.

I hold medicine too sacred to make it a mere ego pursuit.

And yet, that old promise lingers in the back of my mind.

Time will tell. It always does.

For now, you and I will continue these *CannDid Confessions*. And if I don't tell you how it all unfolds, someone else will—long after I'm gone.

[Btw, I just ate that last cookie a few minutes ago. Cannabis is kicking in. Same mellow, smooth high.]

23:54

CHAPTER

48

There's so much left to say. So much left to write. But I don't know if I ever will.

Maybe the universe will conspire for us to meet again—somewhere between the lines of these pages, in the volumes of *CannDid Confessions* yet to come. Maybe the words will flow once more, carrying the weight of thoughts unspoken, of moments not yet lived but waiting to be captured.

For now, though, this was the last cookie. The final bite before I let go for a while. Not forever—no, never that. There will be more journeys, more entheogenic nights, more revelations whispering their truths to me in the silence of the high. There will be more learnings, some gentle, some intense, but always deep. And if fate allows, I'll tell you all about them. As much as I can. Whenever I can.

But tonight... tonight is for feeling. Not for dissecting, not for analyzing, not for turning experience into words. Tonight is just for me—to sink, to dissolve, to trip deeper into myself without needing to put it into sentences. Tonight, I want to *be* before I narrate.

Before I go, though—here's a little something for you. A memory from a different time, a different me.

Did you know I once studied Japanese?

2007.

University days. A different world, a different pace. I fell in love with the script first—the elegance of the kanji, the way each stroke felt like poetry in motion. It was a beautiful language, and I wanted to unravel it, understand its essence, grasp its soul.

I wonder if you can decipher these kanjis I leave for you here. [smiley face]

And even if you can't... don't worry.

I'll tell you all about it one day.

One day.

[even bigger smiley]

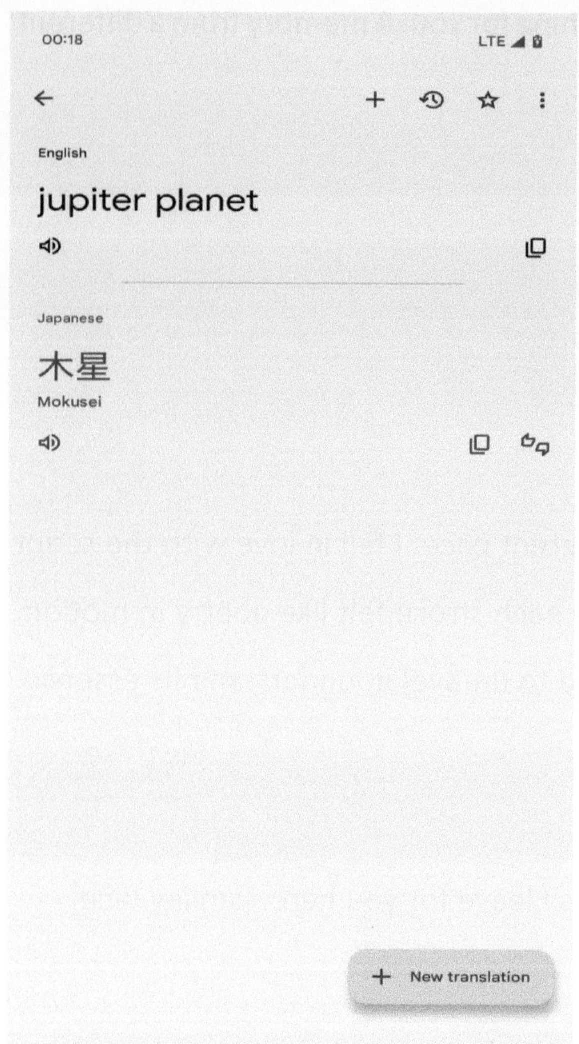

00:18
LTE
English
jupiter planet
Japanese
木星
Mokusei
+ New translation

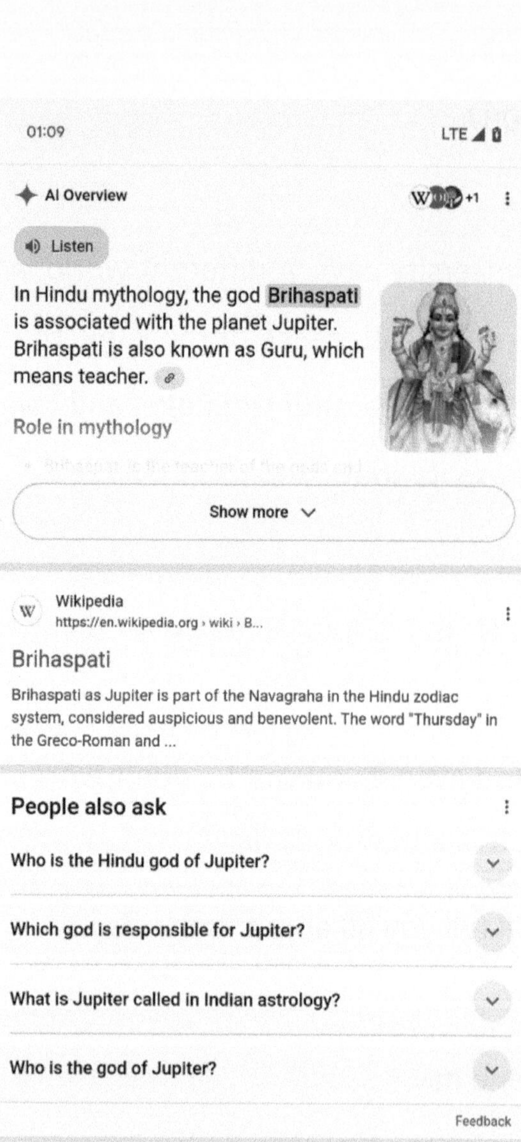

01:09
LTE
✦ AI Overview
+1
Listen
In Hindu mythology, the god Brihaspati is associated with the planet Jupiter. Brihaspati is also known as Guru, which means teacher.
Role in mythology
Show more
Wikipedia
https://en.wikipedia.org › wiki › B...
Brihaspati
Brihaspati as Jupiter is part of the Navagraha in the Hindu zodiac system, considered auspicious and benevolent. The word "Thursday" in the Greco-Roman and ...
People also ask
Who is the Hindu god of Jupiter?
Which god is responsible for Jupiter?
What is Jupiter called in Indian astrology?
Who is the god of Jupiter?
Feedback

.. End of Volume 1 ..

00:25 .. 17 January .. 2025

[Confessions Of A CannDid Mind]

ABOUT THE AUTHOR

Ashish is a nobody.

[No, he really is.]

He has been an educator, a traveler, a student-for-life. He is also a generalist, a human, a (failed) entrepreneur, and a collector of stories.

He loves to delve deep into philosophy and the mysteries of the universe - especially when on entheogens.

He muses about life often trying to find answers to all the existential questions that keep popping into his head from time to time.

He loves to meet new people and bond with likeminded ones - especially over entheogens.

He is a curious experimentalist who hopes to get to know and understand himself even better - especially through his writings, memories, and memoirs - with or without entheogens,

You can find his detailed profile on LinkedIn - https://www.linkedin.com/in/ashish-new/

[If the profile doesn't exist on LinkedIn anymore by the time you look him up - or if LinkedIn has already become extinct by the time you read these words - he can be reached at a.bohora@gmail.com and ashishkdilip@gmail.com if you really, and actually, do want to know more about him]

Printed by Libri Plureos GmbH in Hamburg,
Germany